# THE
# Whole Foods
# *Diabetic*
# Cookbook

**Patricia Bertron**     **Michael Cook**

**Patricia Stevenson**

Book Publishing Company
Summertown, Tennessee

Cover design: Warren Jefferson, Cynthia Holzapfel
Cover Photo: Warren Jefferson
Food Styling: Barbara Bloomfield
Interior design: Gwynelle Dismukes

Printed in Canada

Book Publishing Company
P.O. Box 99
Summertown, TN 38483
1-888-260-8458
www.bookpubco.com

ISBN-13: 978-1-57067-129-6
ISBN-10: 1-57067-129-X

Calculations for the nutritional analyses in this book are based on the average number of servings listed with the recipes and the average amount of an ingredient if a range is called for. Calculations are rounded up to the nearest gram. If two options for an ingredient are listed, the first one is used. Not included are optional ingredients or serving suggestions.

11 10 09 08 07 06      8 7 6 5 4 3

Bertron, Patricia.
   The whole foods diabetic cookbook / Patricia Bertron, Patricia Stevenson, Michael Cook.
      p. cm.
Includes index.
   ISBN 1-57067-129-X
   1. Diabetes--Diet therapy--Recipes. 2. Vegetarian cookery. 3. Natural foods. I. Stevenson, Patricia, 1954- II. Cook, Michael. III. Title.
   RC662 .B42 2002
   641.5'6314--dc21
                            2002002192

# Table of Contents

## WHOLE FOODS RECIPES FOR THE DIABETIC DIET

# THE
# Whole Foods
# *Diabetic*
# Cookbook

*These recipes were created as a way to help people with diabetes incorporate a variety of healthful and flavorful foods in their meal plans. As an added bonus, these dishes will also be tasty additions to any family's menu. These recipes and nutritional information are not in and of themselves intended to be a treatment plan, and they are not intended to replace medical advice.*

# Diabetes – An Overview

## WHAT IS DIABETES?

Diabetes is a disease caused by the inability of the body to produce or properly use insulin. Insulin is a hormone that helps convert sugar, starches, and other food into energy for the body.

There are an estimated 16 million people with diabetes in the United States, almost 6% of the population. The estimated breakdown is 8 million women and 7.5 million men. In this country there are almost 800,000 new cases of diabetes each year. The average age of diagnosis is 46 years, and 49% of those diagnosed have relatives with diabetes. Treating diabetes accounts for about 5% of all health care costs in the United States. Because you can have diabetes with little or no symptoms, about half of the people who currently have diabetes are unaware of it.

You may experience one or more of the following signs and symptoms before you know you have diabetes:

❖ Frequent urination
❖ Extreme thirst
❖ Extreme hunger or fatigue
❖ Dry, itchy skin
❖ Weight loss
❖ Blurred vision
❖ Tingling in the feet or loss of feeling in the feet
❖ Sores that heal slowly

The signs and symptoms of diabetes do not necessarily mean a diagnosis of diabetes. Your doctor can do different types of tests to determine if you have diabetes.

## TYPES OF DIABETES

There are three main types of diabetes. *Type 1* or *insulin-dependent diabetes mellitus* used to be called juvenile-onset diabetes mellitus because most people under 20 who show signs of diabetes have type 1. It affects approximately 5% to 10% of people diagnosed with diabetes. While the causes of type 1 are not completely understood, autoimmune, genetic, and environmental factors are thought to play a part in triggering the disease. People with type 1 diabetes must take insulin in some form because their body no longer makes it.

*Type 2* or *noninsulin-dependent diabetes mellitus* used to be called maturity or adult-onset diabetes mellitus because most people over 30 who are diagnosed with diabetes have type 2. It affects about 90% to 95% of people diagnosed with diabetes. Although most people who develop type 2 diabetes are over 40, it may also affect younger people. With this type of diabetes, the pancreas continues to produce insulin but the cells are resistant to its action. The number of cases of type 2 diabetes are on the rise, possibly related to the large number of overweight and obese people in the United States and how inactive our lifestyle has become. This type of diabetes can begin to occur before any symptoms are noticed. Diet and exercise play strong roles in its management and may possibly help to prevent its development. People with type 2 diabetes may also have to take insulin.

While researchers do not know the exact causes of type 2 diabetes, they do know that it is not caused by eating too much sugar. Having a close relative with type 2 diabetes does increase your chances of developing it yourself, but there are usually other factors that will increase the possibility as well.

A third type of diabetes is called *gestational diabetes mellitus*. It effects about 4% of pregnant women, creating an estimated 135,000 new cases each year. It is thought that hormones released during pregnancy may cause insulin to be less effective. Although gestational diabetes usually diminishes at the end of the pregnancy, more than 50% of the women who incur it will develop type 2 diabetes later in life, particularly if they are overweight or inactive.

About 13.4 million Americans have *impaired fasting glucose levels*. These levels are measurements of the amount of glucose remaining in the body 12 or more hours after eating. Normal fasting blood glucose levels range between 70 and 110 milligrams per deciliter, but with diabetes the levels are much higher. People with above normal fasting blood glucose levels between 110 to 125 mg/dl fall into a category called impaired fasting glucose. This means that their fasting glucose level is above normal but below the level that indicates diabetes (126 mg/dl or greater). Blood glucose levels are checked during a fasting state. You should not eat or drink for a period of time before your blood sugar is checked. Eating or drinking will affect your blood glucose levels. Research continues to be conducted in this area to learn who in this category will actually develop diabetes and how to stop it from happening.

## WHO IS MOST AT RISK FOR TYPE 2 DIABETES?

You are more likely to develop type 2 diabetes if you:
❖ have relatives with diabetes
❖ are overweight
❖ are at least 45 years old
❖ have reduced tolerance to glucose
❖ have high lipid (fat) levels in your blood
❖ have high blood pressure
❖ are Native American, Hispanic, or African American
❖ have had gestational diabetes

Diabetes can be present but undetected for years, causing serious damage to eyes, kidneys, nerves, and blood vessels. Anyone who has symptoms or any of the risk factors should be tested for diabetes.

If you are diagnosed with diabetes, your health care provider may want to monitor other people in your family.

The number of cases of diabetes has grown in every category, but the risk of getting type 2 diabetes at an earlier age is dramatically on the rise. From 1990 to 1998 the incidence of diabetes in people in their 30s rose 70%. Many doctors recommend that people with risk factors be tested for diabetes at age 30 so that treatment, if necessary, can begin and patients can stay healthier longer.

## COMPLICATIONS OF DIABETES

Poor control over diabetes can lead to other health problems. However, learning to manage your diabetes can help to reduce your risk of experiencing complications. A vegetarian diet can be an important component of an effective treatment plan.

### High Blood Pressure

Rates of hypertension in people with diabetes are double that of the nondiabetic population. High blood pressure occurs more often as we age. About 30% to 75% of the complications that occur with diabetes are because of high blood pressure.

Individuals who follow a vegetarian diet generally have lower blood pressure than meat eaters do. Although no one knows for sure why this is so, some studies have shown that meat consumption increases blood pressure. Vegetarians generally have lower blood cholesterol levels and lower rates of hypertension, which also helps reduce the risk of developing cardiovascular disease later in life. High blood pressure may also increase the risk of developing kidney disease. Diet, exercise, and medication can all help to bring blood pressure under control.

Reducing sodium intake is an important step to take to lower blood pressure. Many processed foods are high in sodium. Preparing your own meals can give you greater control over your sodium intake. The sodium content is given in all the recipes in this book. As with other adjustments in eating, as you reduce the amount of sodium in your diet, you will become used to eating foods that are less salty and will probably become more aware of the other flavors your food has to offer.

## Heart Disease

More than half the people with diabetes die from the complications of cardiovascular disease. Diabetes mellitus is one of the major risk factors for cardiovascular disease.

An extensive body of research confirms the strong favorable effect plant-based diets have on heart disease risk reduction. (Brenda Davis and Vesanto Melina, *Becoming Vegan,* Book Publishing Company, Summertown, Tenn., 2000, page 20.)

Blood cholesterol levels play an important role in the risk of heart disease. One of the main goals of diabetes management is to achieve and maintain good blood cholesterol levels. High intakes of cholesterol and saturated fat can increase the risk for developing heart disease. Vegan and vegetarian diets tend to be lower in saturated fat than nonvegetarian diets.

For every 1% drop in blood cholesterol, the risk of developing heart disease decreases by 3% to 4%. Vegan diets contain no cholesterol, and one study found blood cholesterol levels of vegans were 35% lower than those of nonvegetarians.

Vegetarian diets are high in the antioxidant vitamins E, and C, beta-carotene, and phytochemicals, which play protective roles in reducing the risk of heart disease.

## Kidney Disease

Diabetes is the most common cause of kidney failure, often called *end-stage renal disease* (ESRD). People with diabetes account for one-third of all cases of ESRD in the United States. Possible reasons are that people with diabetes are living longer; the number of people being diagnosed with diabetes is increasing; and people with diabetes and ESRD are being treated in ESRD programs that have previously excluded them. Of individuals with type 1 or type 2 diabetes, approximately 20% to 30% will develop ESRD.

Vegetarian diets may be beneficial in reducing the risk of developing kidney disease, because they tend to be lower in protein, which can help reduce the progression of this disease. Diets high in protein can have a negative effect on the kidneys. The type of protein eaten is also an important consideration. Plant proteins have been shown to reduce the amount of protein in the urine and blood flow through the kidneys. This may cause less damage to tissues in the kidneys than animal protein.

## Eye Problems

People with diabetes may also experience problems with their eyes called *retinopathy*. It is the primary cause of blindness in adults aged 20 to 74 years in the United States. The longer a person has diabetes, the more likely they are to develop eye problems. High blood pressure and high blood sugar are risk factors for developing eye problems.

# *Controlling Diabetes with Diet and Exercise*

## HEALTH BENEFITS OF A VEGETARIAN DIET

There is a strong and consistent message about diet which has been demonstrated by many years of solid scientific research: Animal-centered diets increase the risk of chronic diseases; plant-centered diets, low in saturated fat and cholesterol, and rich in dietary fiber and phytochemicals, decrease the risk of these diseases. (*Becoming Vegan*, page 19.)

If you have diabetes, following a vegetarian diet can provide you with many health advantages which may reduce the risk of developing complications of diabetes later in life. A whole foods vegetarian diet can be beneficial in many ways. It can play an important role in helping control blood sugar levels. In addition, people with type 2 diabetes need to reach and maintain a healthful weight and achieve normal blood fat levels and blood pressure. A well-designed vegetarian diet can be beneficial in reaching all of those goals.

## Good Reasons to Eat Vegetarian

The outlook for a person with diabetes is much brighter if they learn to maintain good control of their diet and lifestyle. A great deal of research is being done on the benefits of diet and exercise in managing, and in some cases improving, the health of people with diabetes.

One such pilot study conducted by the Physicians Committee for Responsible Medicine and Georgetown University Medical Center in Washington, D.C., looked at how a low-fat vegan diet (no meat, eggs, or dairy products) for people with type 2 diabetes could lower cholesterol and blood glucose levels. Participants were assigned to two groups. The first group followed a low-fat vegan diet which allowed unlimited portions of vegetables, fruits, whole grains, and legumes. The use of oil was kept to a bare minimum and refined breads and pasta were replaced with whole grain sources of those foods. All meals were cholesterol-free and provided about 60 to 70 grams of fiber per day.

The second group followed a conventional low-fat diet that was more in line with the American Dietetic Association guidelines. Those diets were higher in fat and included about 30 grams of fiber and 200 milligrams of cholesterol per day.

Participants attended classes twice a week for support and instruction on nutrition and cooking. The study lasted 12 weeks. Results showed that average blood glucose levels decreased 28% in the vegan group compared with 12% in the conventional group. The use of medication decreased in the vegan group but remained unchanged in the conventional group. The vegan group also had more substantial drops in their cholesterol levels compared with the conventional group. Finally, the vegan group lost an average of about 16 pounds compared with a loss of about 8 pounds in the conventional group.

The results of this study are promising. It demonstrates that a vegan diet can improve the health of people with diabetes. The benefits of a vegan diet in improving diabetes control deserves further research with a larger number of study participants.

## Different Types of Vegetarians

There are many types of vegetarian diets. Individuals generally choose to follow a vegetarian diet because of health, ethical, environmental, or religious reasons. Three of the main types of vegetarian diets are described below.

Strict vegetarians or *vegans* eat fruits, vegetables, grains, and legumes and avoid all animal products, including meat, poultry, fish, eggs, dairy products, and honey. The recipes in this book are all vegan.

*Lacto-vegetarians* eat dairy products, plant foods, and avoid all other animal products.

*Lacto-ovo-vegetarians* consume eggs, dairy products, and plant foods and avoid meat, poultry, and fish.

Unfortunately, much of the nonvegetarian public thinks vegetarians survive on meals of lettuce and broccoli with a few nuts and seeds thrown in for good measure. But this is not true. The plant kingdom contains an enormous variety of foods which can be prepared and combined in a great many ways. In general, vegetarians may be more health conscious than the general public and more concerned with proper nutrition and avoiding processed foods, but this does not mean they are living a deprived existence. As you will see from the recipes in this book, a vegetarian diet provides a variety of colorful, flavorful, and nutritious foods.

## Learning What Works for You

Each person who develops diabetes will have their own unique response to diet and exercise. Learning how your body handles various foods and the amount of activity you engage in is a critical part of learning to manage your diabetes. In consultation with doctors, dieticians, and diabetic counselors, you can develop a plan that is just right for you. These recipes and menu plans contain a range of carbohydrates that will allow you to incorporate them into any meal plan. Include your family and friends in your new adventures in eating. Talk to your health care team about creating a vegetarian diet that works for you.

Like anything else, learning to eat differently will require some effort. Just the thought may seem a little overwhelming, but there is good news. It takes about three to six weeks for a new routine to become a regular habit. If you really stick to your new diet during that time, you will be surprised at how natural it will seem.

Enjoy your exploration of new foods, and share the experience with your family and friends. Remember that what you are trying to achieve is a life-long transformation to optimize your health.

## MAINTAINING A HEALTHY WEIGHT

Obesity is one of the main risk factors for developing type 2 diabetes. About half of all Americans are overweight or obese. This is much higher than the previous decade. A vegetarian diet alone can make a tremendous difference in the amount of weight gain you experience. Vegetarians tend to be leaner than nonvegetarians and weigh about 10 to 20 pounds less than lacto-ovo-vegetarians.

### Exercise

Physical activity is an important part of diabetes management. Exercise provides many health benefits, including improved blood glucose control, which can decrease the need for medication.

Other benefits of exercise include:

❖ Decreased blood cholesterol which can lower the risk for developing heart disease
❖ Improved blood pressure control
❖ Improved physical fitness
❖ Decreased stress
❖ Increased self-esteem
❖ Decreased depression

When you are beginning an exercise program, find something you enjoy. Get your family and friends involved. If you have support and are engaged in a variety of activities you enjoy, you are much more likely to stick with them. Staying active is a vital part of staying healthy for anyone. Whether you enjoy walking, gardening, swimming, or doing housework, all types of activity can count as some form of exercise.

Before starting any exercise program, be sure to get the seal of approval from your doctor. You might need to be screened for health complications that may make some forms of exercise difficult or risky for you to do. Depending on your type of diabetes and level of activity, you may need to adjust your diet and medications.

If you have type 1 diabetes, you will need to adjust your diet and medications in order to exercise safely. Be aware that your glycogen stores, blood insulin levels, nutritional status, and fitness level can effect your blood sugar response to exercise. Check your blood sugar levels before and after you exercise and keep a record of them. Let your doctor know about your levels so your medication can be adjusted as necessary.

If you have type 1 diabetes, you need to prevent hypoglycemia (low blood sugar) during or after exercise. This can occur due to eating too little, taking too much medication, or exercising more than usual. Table 1 provides some guidelines on how to help control your blood sugar response to exercise.

If you have type 2 diabetes, exercise can help to control your blood sugar and improve insulin sensitivity. Since these effects only last up to 72 hours after your last exercise session, it is important to maintain a consistent

---

**Table 1**
**Managing Your Blood Sugar Response to Exercise**

❖ Avoid exercise if your fasting blood sugar level is above 250 mg/dl and ketosis is present.

❖ Be cautious if your blood sugar level is greater than 300 mg/dl without the presence of ketosis.

❖ Monitor your blood sugar before and after exercise.

❖ Try to pinpoint when food patterns or insulin may need to be changed.

❖ Learn your body's response to exercise.

❖ Consume additional carbohydrate-rich foods as necessary to avoid hypoglycemia.

| Table 2 | |
| --- | --- |
| **Cardiovascular** | **Resistance** |
| Walking | Lifting weights |
| Cycling | Crunches |
| Running | Rowing machine |
| Dancing | Squat, lunge |
| Aerobics | Push-ups |

exercise program in order to continue to receive these benefits. If you do not have significant complications or limitations, work towards a goal of doing a combination of resistance and cardiovascular exercises. This can help to improve cardiovascular fitness, encourage weight loss, and increase muscle strength and endurance, as well as improve your blood sugar and blood cholesterol levels. Table 2 lists various cardiovascular and resistance exercises.

Hypoglycemia does not usually occur in people with type 2 diabetes, but it can if you are taking sulfonylurea medication or insulin and exercising for a long period of time. You should monitor your blood sugar levels before and after you exercise to be sure you are in good blood control.

It is important to take good care of your feet during exercise. Wearing sneakers that contain silica gel or air midsoles along with wearing polyester or cotton-polyester socks will help prevent blisters and keep your feet dry. This is especially important if you have a type of nerve damage called *peripheral neuropathy* that reduces sensation in the feet.

It is best to start your workout with a warm up, followed by stretching, and then gradually increase the intensity of your exercise. Once you finish walking, swimming—whatever your chosen activity—gradually slow your pace and do a cool down for 5 to 10 minutes, consisting of exercises you would do during warm up. This will help to bring your heart rate down to its pre-exercise level.

Before, during, and after exercise, it is important to drink plenty of fluids. Consume two cups of water or other drink approximately two hours prior to exercise in order to ensure that your body is adequately hydrated. It will also give your body time to eliminate any excess fluid. During exercise, consume fluids frequently in order to replace those lost through sweating. After exercise, consume two cups of fluid for every pound of weight lost during exercise. A good way to judge weight loss during exercise is to use a scale before and after exercise to measure your difference in weight.

Remember the body's response to exercise is complex and will vary with each individual. While some rules of thumb may be handy, they are no substitute for consulting with your doctor and conducting careful monitoring.

## DEALING WITH STRESS

Everyone has some stress in his or her life. It can make control of diabetes more difficult. People under stress may find it harder to get organized and do all the things that are necessary to ensure good health. Hormones released during stress may directly alter blood sugar levels. In people with type 2 diabetes, stress often raises blood sugar levels. Reducing stress can help anyone with diabetes take better care of themselves.

Consult with your health care team about strategies for reducing stress. There are many fine resources available to teach you simple, effective ways of doing this. Breathing techniques, relaxation therapy, and exercise can help you learn how to relax even in difficult situations. While relaxation techniques will probably be more beneficial to people with type 2 diabetes, reducing stress can also help people with type 1 take better care of themselves.

Finding a support group can help relieve the feeling of being alone. You can also learn from the coping strategies that other people use.

In the next chapter, you'll see how you can get the nutritional support you need to maintain a healthy body weight and good metabolism from a vegetarian diet.

# Meeting Nutrient Needs

## COUNTING CALORIES, CARBS, PROTEIN, AND FAT

While each person needs to develop an individual diet plan along with their health care team, here are some guidelines to help you make informed choices about which foods are best for you. Table 3 on the next page shows how many calories you should get on a daily basis from protein, carbohydrates, and fat. Table 4 gives you the number of calories per gram for protein, carbohydrates, and fat. Table 5 then gives you the formula to determine what percentage of calories in a given food come from protein, carbohydrates, and fat. For example, if you and your health care consultant decide that no more than 25% of your calories should come from fat, you will be able to select the foods that will help you to meet that goal.

## Table 3
## Recommended Distribution of Calories from Protein, Carbohydrates, and Fat

| Nutrient | % of Total |
|----------|------------|
| Calories | |
| Carbohydrates | 50-60% |
| Protein | 10-20% |
| Fat | |
| Total | 20-30% |
| Saturated fat | less than 7% |
| Essential fatty acids | |
| Linoleic | 2-3% |
| Alpha-linoleic | 1% |

## Table 4
## Calculating the Number of Calories in a Food

| | Calories per gram |
|---|---|
| Carbohydrates | 4 |
| Protein | 4 |
| Fats | 9 |
| Alcohol | 7 |

## Table 5
## To figure out the percentage of carbohydrates, protein, or fat in a food:

1. MULTIPLY the number of grams of carbohydrates, protein, or fat times the calories per gram for that nutrient. (See table 4.)

2. DIVIDE the total calories of that nutrient by the total number of calories in the food. The answer is the percentage of carbohydrates, protein, or fat in the recipe.

### Example:

If a food contains 100 calories made up of 15 grams of carbohydrates, 5 grams of protein, and 2 grams of fat, then:

15 g carbohydrates x 4 calories per gram　　= 60 calories

60 calories divided by 100 total calories　　= 60% of calories from carbohydrates

## Carbohydrates

Carbohydrates are the body's main source of energy and are divided into two groups: complex and simple. Starches and fiber are complex carbohydrates. Beans, grains, and some vegetables are good sources of starches, while fiber is found in those foods plus fruits, nuts, and seeds.

Sugars are simple carbohydrates and are found in fruits and other plant foods. Fructose is the sugar found naturally in fruits, and sucrose is another type of sugar that is found in some fruits and vegetables. Other sources of simple sugars are listed in Table 6. About 50% to 60% of your calories should come from carbohydrates, with an emphasis on complex carbohydrates.

Unlike animal foods, which are devoid of carbohydrates, plant foods are excellent sources of this essential nutrient. Research has demonstrated that diets high in complex carbohydrates can increase a person's ability to respond to insulin. In general, the closer a food is to its natural state, the higher it will be in complex carbohydrates. For example, brown rice is the entire grain with only the inedible outer husk removed. To make white

| Table 6 |
| :---: |
| **Sources of Simple Sugars** |
| table sugar (sucrose) |
| maple syrup |
| brown sugar |
| raw sugar |
| corn syrup |
| cane sugar |
| confectioner's sugar |
| dextrin |
| high fructose corn syrup |
| molasses |
| honey |
| turbinado sugar |
| fructose |
| maltose |
| lactose (cow's milk sugar) |

rice, the bran and germ are removed as well. This not only reduces the amount of complex carbohydrates, but also causes some important nutrients to be lost during processing. Some good sources of complex carbohydrates are shown in Table 7.

Diets higher in refined carbohydrates, such as white bread, pasta, pretzels, and plain bagels, can cause elevations in glucose and fat levels.

Sugar is no longer strictly banned for people with diabetes. It has been shown that sugar does not raise blood glucose levels more quickly than many other carbohydrates. However, the more sugar you eat the more likely it is that you will eat less nutritious foods. Sugar is also frequently present in high-fat, low-fiber foods that do not supply necessary nutrients. If you eat some foods with sugar, you need to determine your own glycemic response to them.

Meals containing whole grains, beans, and vegetables are satisfying and filling. Fruits supply nutrients and can satisfy cravings for sweetness. As you shift your diet to reduce sweets and include more fruit, you will find that you become more sensitive to lower levels of sweetness and will require less to satisfy your needs.

| **Table 7**<br>**Food Sources of**<br>**Complex Carbohydrates** |
| :---: |
| barley |
| black beans |
| buckwheat |
| bulgur |
| chick-peas |
| corn |
| kamut |
| millet |
| navy beans |
| peas |
| pinto beans |
| quinoa |
| wheat berries |
| whole grain breads and pasta |

## Protein

Protein is a component of muscles, bones, and hormones and is needed to produce enzymes. It is also used by the body to build, repair, and maintain tissues. Some amino acids—the building blocks of protein—can be made by the body. These are called *nonessential amino acids*. The ones your body cannot make are called *essential amino acids* and need to come from your diet.

You can get all the protein you need by eating a variety of plant foods throughout the day. Certain plant foods complement each other's amino acid composition, making complete proteins which contain all of the essential amino acids. In general, beans with grains or beans with nuts provide complete protein, but they do not necessarily have to be eaten at the same meal. Soybeans provide complete protein on their own.

Vegetarian diets contain excellent protein foods. For people with diabetes, 10% to 20% of their daily calorie intake should be from protein. Some good sources of protein are listed in Table 8 on the next page. (If you have kidney disease, consult with your doctor about the proper level of protein intake.)

## Fats

Fats are essential nutrients. A layer of fat under the skin provides insulation. Fats cushion the vital organs, provide reserve energy, and store the fat-soluble vitamins, among other functions.

Fat is digested more slowly than other nutrients, so its presence delays the return of hunger. However, fats also increase the number of calories that a food provides. The key to smart fat consumption is to limit the types and amounts. Eating a low-fat diet is important for the person with diabetes for several reasons. When consumed in large amounts, dietary fat can greatly impact the management of diabetes by interfering with the way insulin does its job. Keeping fat intake low is one of the best ways to lose weight and keep it off. A low-fat diet can be important in avoiding strokes and heart attacks, some of the most serious complications associated with diabetes.

Limiting the amounts of saturated animal fat and cholesterol in your diet can help reduce your risk of developing heart disease.

### Table 8
### Selected Food Sources of Protein

| Food | Amount | Protein (g) |
|------|--------|-------------|
| Chick-peas, boiled | 1 cup | 14.5 |
| Black beans, boiled | 1 cup | 15.2 |
| Lentils, boiled | 1 cup | 17.9 |
| Peanut butter | 2 Tbsp | 8.0 |
| Quinoa, cooked | 1 cup | 11.0 |
| Bulgur, cooked | 1 cup | 5.6 |
| Whole wheat bread | 1 slice | 2.7 |
| Tofu, firm | ½ cup | 19.9 |
| Tempeh | ½ cup | 15.7 |
| Seitan* | 4 ounces | 24.0 |
| Spinach, boiled | 1 cup | 5.4 |
| Broccoli | 1 cup | 4.6 |

*Source: Pennington JAT. Bowes and Church's Food Values of Portions Commonly Used. Harper and Row, New York, 1998. *Manufacturers information.*

One gram of fat, regardless of the source, provides nine calories. That is more than double the calories you would get from consuming a gram of carbohydrate or protein. Limit fat intake to no more than 20% to 30% of calories. If you are trying to lose weight, staying at the lower level will greatly increase your chances of success. Table 9 shows some sources of fat in the diet.

The three main types of fat are saturated, polyunsaturated, and monounsaturated fat. *Saturated fat* is solid at room temperature and is found primarily in animal products. Plant-based foods generally contain very little saturated fat compared with animal products. Coconut and palm oils contain saturated vegetable fat, but this does not cause the type of health problems that saturated animal fats do. Consumption of saturated animal fat is linked

**Table 9**
**Sources of Fat in the Diet**

| Type of Fat | Primary Food Sources |
| --- | --- |
| Saturated animal fat | Meat, poultry, whole dairy products, eggs, butter, lard |
| Saturated vegetable fat | Palm oil, palm kernel oil, and coconut oil |
| Monounsaturated fat | Avocados, canola oil, nuts, olives, and olive oil |
| Polyunsaturated fat | Safflower oil, sunflower oil, and corn oil |
| Linoleic acid (Omega-6) | Sunflower, safflower, corn, and grape seed oils, grains, walnuts, seeds such as pumpkin and sesame seeds |
| Alpha-linoleic acid (Omega-3) | Flaxseed, hempseed, canola oil, soybeans, walnuts, and dark green leafy vegetables |

with an increased risk of heart disease and cancer. It should be limited to no more than 7% of your calories.

*Monounsaturated fats* are generally semisolid when refrigerated and liquid at room temperature. In moderation they are beneficial to people with diabetes for improving blood sugar levels. These fats may help to lower total blood cholesterol levels without reducing HDL (the "good" cholesterol) and have not been found to increase the risk for developing cancer.

*Polyunsaturated fats* are liquid at room temperature and do not become solid when refrigerated.

*Linoleic acid* (an omega-6 fatty acid) and *alpha-linoleic acid* (an omega-3 fatty acid) are polyunsaturated fats that your body cannot manufacture on its own. They are called essential fatty acids, which means they need to come from foods you eat. Both are necessary for the formation of healthy cell membranes. They are also important to the development and functioning of the brain and nervous system, and are essential in the production of substances that regulate many vital organ systems. It is important to have a balance of these fats. The National Institutes of Health suggest 2% to 3% of your total calories come from linoleic acid and 1% of total calories come from alpha-linoleic acid. In a diet of 2,400 calories per day, that would mean about 72 calories (8 g) of linoleic acid and 24 calories (2.6 g) of alpha-linoleic acid. Food sources of these fatty acids are listed in Table 9 on page 31.

You should be aware of another type of fat called *trans-fatty acids*. These are produced when unsaturated fats are put through a process called hydrogenation, which makes them harder. Most margarine and vegetable shortening contain *hydrogenated* fats. Try to avoid foods that are processed with hydrogenated or partially hydrogenated vegetable oils. Examples include cookies, crackers, cakes and pastries, peanut butter, and fast foods. Hydrogenated fats can increase your risk of developing heart disease and can interfere with the normal function of some fats. Currently, manufacturers are not required to list the amount of trans fats in a food product. But you can calculate the amount as long as the nutrition

---

### Table 10
### Calculating Trans Fats in a Food Product

| Example: | Margarine |
|---|---|
| Serving size: | 1 tablespoon |
| Total fat: | 14 grams |
| Saturated fat: | 2 grams |
| Monounsaturated fat: | 6 grams |
| Polyunsaturated fat: | 4 grams |

Step 1: Add together the saturated, mono-unsaturated, and polyunsaturated fats.

| Saturated | 2 grams |
|---|---|
| Mono | 6 grams |
| Poly | 4 grams |
| Total: | 12 grams |

Step 2: Subtract the total for the saturated, monounsaturated, and polyunsaturated fats from the total fat. This will give you the number of trans-fatty acids in the margarine.

| Total fat | 14 grams |
|---|---|
| Step 1 total | -12 grams |
| Total trans fats | 2 grams |

label lists the amount of saturated, polyunsaturated, mono-unsaturated and total fat on the food label. Table 10 on page 33 provides an example of how to calculate the trans-fatty acid content of a food product.

## FIBER

Fiber is only found in plant foods. It is the part of the plant that can not be completely digested and passes intact through the digestive tract. It provides bulk, which helps prevent constipation. Fiber does not supply any calories. Vegetarian diets based on whole foods are rich in fiber—double or triple that of a typical nonvegetarian diet. Research suggests that diets high in fiber may be associated with reduced insulin requirements in people with diabetes and may help protect against the development of type 2 diabetes.

There are two types of fiber. *Soluble fiber* found in fruits, vegetables, barley, legumes, oats, and oat bran may be helpful in controlling blood glucose levels. It is called soluble because it absorbs water during digestion, taking on a gel-like consistency. Some types of soluble fiber can impede the absorption of glucose from the small intestines after eating. This helps keep blood glucose levels under control and can decrease the need for insulin. Soluble fiber has the added benefit of helping manage blood fat levels, reducing the risk for cardiovascular disease.

*Insoluble fiber* is found in fruits, vegetables, cereals, whole-grain products, and wheat bran. Unlike soluble fiber, which can dissolve in water, insoluble fiber retains its basic structure during digestion and holds onto water, helping to prevent constipation.

Both types of fiber help fill you up without adding calories. As you add more fiber to your diet, you should increase the amount of water you drink to help your body effectively use the fiber.

Fruits, vegetables, grains, and legumes are all good sources of fiber. Aim for at least 20 to 35 grams of fiber per day. When reading food labels, try to find foods that have at least 5 grams of fiber per serving. See Table 11 on page 36 for the fiber content of some foods.

## MINERALS AND VITAMINS IN A VEGETARIAN DIET

A well-balanced vegetarian diet supplies all of the necessary minerals, trace minerals, and vitamins. The key is to eat a variety of whole foods on a regular basis. There are a few key nutrients that people may be concerned about getting in a vegetarian diet. Understanding their importance and the variety of plant sources of those nutrients can help create a nutritious diet.

### Calcium

Calcium is a mineral that is necessary for building strong bones and teeth. It also aids in muscle contraction. About 99% of the body's calcium is stored in the bones while 1% circulates in the blood. A commonly expressed

# Table 11
## Selected Food Sources of Fiber

| Food | Amount | Fiber (g) | Food | Amount | Fiber (g) |
|---|---|---|---|---|---|
| **GRAINS** | | | **VEGETABLES** | | |
| Bulgur, cooked | 1 cup | 8.2 | Broccoli, boiled | ½ cup | 2.3 |
| Barley, pearled, cooked | 1 cup | 6.0 | Brussels sprouts, boiled | ½ cup | 2.0 |
| Millet, cooked | 1 cup | 3.1 | Carrots, boiled | ½ cup | 2.6 |
| Oatmeal, quick, cooked | 1 cup | 4.0 | Collard greens, boiled, chopped | 1 cup | 3.6 |
| Quinoa | ½ cup | 5.0 | Corn, boiled | ½ cup | 2.3 |
| Kellogg's All Bran | ½ cup | 10.0 | Green beans, boiled | ½ cup | 2.0 |
| Kellogg's Corn flakes | 1 cup | 1.1 | Peas, green, boiled | ½ cup | 4.4 |
| Nabisco Shredded Wheat N' Bran | 1½ cups | 8.0 | Spinach, boiled | ½ cup | 2.2 |
| Oat bran, raw | ⅓ cup | 4.8 | Tomato, red, raw | 1 | 1.4 |
| Wheat bran | ½ cup | 6.4 | **LEGUMES** | | |
| Wheat germ | ½ cup | 3.8 | Baked beans | 1 cup | 13.9 |
| **FRUITS** | | | Beans, vegetarian | 1 cup | 12.7 |
| Apple | 1 medium | 3.7 | Black beans, boiled | 1 cup | 15.0 |
| Banana | 1 medium | 2.7 | Chick-peas, boiled | 1 cup | 12.5 |
| Orange | 1 | 3.1 | Kidney beans, red, boiled | 1 cup | 13.1 |
| Pear | 1 medium | 4.0 | Lentils, boiled | 1 cup | 15.6 |
| Prunes, dried | 5 | 3.0 | Navy beans, boiled | 1 cup | 11.6 |
| Strawberries | 1 cup | 3.4 | Soybeans, green, boiled | 1 cup | 7.6 |

Source: Pennington JAT. Bowes and Church's Food Values of Portions Commonly Used. Harper and Row, New York, 1998.

concern when people change to a vegan diet is where will they get calcium if they aren't consuming dairy products?

The level of calcium in your body is not simply a matter of how much you take in but also how much you keep. There is a complex interplay of intake, absorption, and excretion. (*Becoming Vegan*, page 93.)

Protein and sodium content in the diet play key roles in the absorption and excretion of calcium. Diets that are low in sodium and do not contain excessive amounts of protein (particularly animal protein) can increase the amount of calcium you absorb and retain.

Because the need for calcium has so many variables, determining the amount required at any stage of life can be difficult. The current recommendation for people age 19 to 50 is 1,000 mg per day and for people over 50, it is 1,200 mg per day.

Calcium is found in a variety of plant foods. Dark green, leafy vegetables are one excellent source of calcium (with the exception of spinach, which is higher in oxalic acid, a substance that inhibits the absorption of calcium). Other good sources include beans, calcium-fortified soymilk and juices, and tofu produced with calcium. Table 12 shows the calcium content of some plant foods.

| Table 12 Calcium Amounts | | |
|---|---|---|
| Food | Serving Size | Calcium |
| Broccoli | ½ cup | 36 mg |
| Kale | ½ cup | 47 mg |
| White beans | 1 cup | 162 mg |
| Pinto beans | 1 cup | 82 mg |
| Tofu with calcium | ½ cup | 471 mg |
| Sweet potatoes | ½ cup | 27 mg |
| Cow's milk | ½ cup | 135 mg |

## Zinc

Zinc is an important constituent of insulin. It is involved in over 60 separate enzyme systems and plays a role in cell growth. Zinc is involved in the immune system, blood formation, and the development of new proteins. Phytates, fiber, calcium, and protein all have an impact on zinc absorption and utilization. Vegetarians tend to consume less than the Recommended Daily Allowance (12 mg for women; 15 mg for men) but can still obtain adequate amounts of this nutrient by consuming a variety of zinc-rich foods. Good sources include some breakfast cereals (Grape-Nuts, bran flakes, instant oatmeal), legumes, nuts, soy products, and sea vegetables.

## Iron

Iron is responsible for the formation of hemoglobin in the blood and myoglobin in the muscles, which supply oxygen to the cells. Good plant-based sources of iron include green, leafy vegetables, soy foods, legumes, nuts, whole-grain breads, fortified breads, cereals, and pasta. Vitamin C, when consumed in the same meal as these foods, greatly enhances the absorption of iron, particularly in individuals who are iron deficient. Some foods are naturally rich in vitamin C and iron, such as Swiss chard, spinach, broccoli, other dark green vegetables, and vitamin C-rich breakfast cereals.

### Vitamin B$_{12}$

Vitamin B$_{12}$ is only produced by microorganisms. The recommended daily intake is from 2 to 2.8 mcg. Although this is a very small amount, it is absolutely essential. A little B$_{12}$ is stored in the body, but getting some in your diet each week is important for good health.

Diets that include meat or dairy contain B$_{12}$. Vegans require B$_{12}$ in the form of a supplement or fortified food. Some sources are fortified cereals, fortified soymilk, Red Star Nutritional Support Formula nutritional yeast, and vitamin supplements. It is best to get your B$_{12}$ in small doses on a regular basis. Large, single doses cannot be retained. Getting enough B$_{12}$ is important for everyone, but it is particularly important during pregnancy, infancy, early childhood, and the later years.

### Artificial Sweeteners

According to a government survey called the Continuing Survey of Food Intakes by Individuals (1994-1996), the average American consumes the equivalent of approximately 20 teaspoons of sugar a day, which adds up to about 300 calories. Over a week, that's an additional 2,100 calories which can replace valuable nutrients in your diet, not to mention the effect it can have on your blood sugar level. Most of this comes from sweetened beverages. After that, table sugar is a significant source; a smaller amount comes from other sweeteners, like honey and molasses.

Artificial sweeteners are used as an alternative to sugar in diet soda, baked goods, and many other products. Four sugar substitutes have been approved by the Food and Drug Administration (FDA) for use in various foods: saccharin, aspartame, acesulfame-K, and sucralose. All four are considered to be vegan. Table 13 lists some of the other names under which these products are sold. According to the American Dietetic Association's position paper on the use of nutritive and nonnutritive sweeteners: "Nonnutritive sweeteners are also appropriate in meal plans for persons with diabetes and may help [with] control of energy intake."

**Acesulfame-K** is about 200 times sweeter than sucrose (table sugar). It is calorie-free and therefore does not affect blood sugar levels. It is used as a tabletop sweetener and may be found as an additive to chewing gum, confections, desserts, yogurts, sauces, and alcoholic beverages. Many of these products may not be vegan, so be sure to read the ingredient label on the package.

**Aspartame** is 160 to 220 times sweeter than sucrose. Although it does provide 4 calories per kilogram, the

| Table 13 Artificial Sweeteners | |
|---|---|
| **Sweetener** | **Other names** |
| Acesulfame-K | Sunett |
| Aspartame | Equal, Nutrasweet |
| Saccharin | Sweet and Low |
| Sucralose | Splenda |

intense sweetness of this product results in a negligible amount of energy being derived from its use. Some concern has been expressed over the years regarding its safety. Since it was approved in 1981, the FDA has evaluated its use in foods and beverages 26 times and in 1996 approved it as a general-purpose sweetener for use in various foods and beverages. One of the breakdown products of aspartame is phenylalanine, which cannot be metabolized by individuals with phenylketonuria. Therefore, the FDA requires that foods containing this sweetener contain a label stating that they contain phenylalanine.

**Saccharin** is about 200 to 700 times sweeter than sucrose. It is calorie free and does not effect blood sugar levels. Since some studies have found it to be a carcinogen in rats, products containing saccharin must contain the warning: "Use of this product may be hazardous to your health. This product contains saccharin which has been determined to cause cancer in laboratory animals." Also, the amount of saccharin in a product must be included on the food label and cannot exceed 12 milligrams per ounce in beverages, 20 milligrams per sweetening equivalent of 1 teaspoon of sugar, or not greater than 30 milligrams per serving of food.

**Sucralose** is about 600 times sweeter than sucrose. It does not provide energy, cannot be digested, and is excreted in the urine. Sucralose is made from table sugar and therefore tastes a lot like it. Because its sweetness is much more intense than sugar, it is bulked up with maltodextrin, a starchy powder, so it can be measured out more like sugar. The FDA has approved its use as a general-purpose sweetener in foods.

Another product, **stevia**, deserves mention here. It is derived from a shrub called *Stevia rebaudiana (Bertoni)* found in Paraguay and Brazil. It has been used in the treatment of diabetes among native peoples in these countries, although exactly how it lowers blood sugar levels is unknown. Stevia has a sweet taste but has not been approved by the FDA as a food additive. However, it can be sold as a "dietary supplement."

## EXCHANGE LISTS FOR MEAL PLANNING

So far we have covered general recommendations for people with diabetes. Your needs will vary based upon your type of diabetes, use of medications, level of activity, and other health conditions or complications. You may wish to consult with a registered dietitian to develop an individualized meal plan that best meets your needs.

The Exchange Lists for Meal Planning were developed by the American Dietetic Association and the American Diabetes Association to educate people with diabetes on how to count calories and how to choose foods that best meet their needs. The exchange lists are divided into seven groups: starch, fruit, milk, vegetables, other carbohydrates, meat and meat substitutes, and fat. The serving sizes for foods listed within each of these food groups all have about the same number of calories, carbohydrates, protein, and fat. The exceptions are the milk and meat and meat substitute groups, which are further broken down into smaller categories based on the fat content of the foods listed. (The complete booklet can be purchased through the American Dietetic Association, Chicago, Il.)

Exchange lists may be helpful when trying to achieve a certain calorie level and nutrient intake; however, they do not include some foods typically used by vegans. A few adjustments are necessary to account for meat-free, dairy-free diets.

For the **milk group**, low-fat fortified soymilk or soy yogurt can be used in place of cow's milk or yogurt.

For the **starch list**, $\frac{1}{3}$ cup cooked millet, quinoa, or wheat berries equals one starch exchange. Sea vegetables and alfalfa sprouts can be added to the vegetable list, with one exchange equaling $\frac{1}{2}$ cup cooked or 1 cup raw.

The **meat and meat substitutes** group already includes some soyfoods, and beans, peas, and lentils. The following items are not included in the exchange lists but have the same amount of protein as one meat exchange:

2 ounces tempeh
1 ounce seitan
$\frac{1}{4}$ cup roasted soy nuts
$\frac{1}{4}$ cup rehydrated textured vegetable protein
2 ounces soy burger
1 ounce soy hot dog

Each contains 7 grams of protein. The calories, carbohydrate, and fat content of each item will vary.

Additional fat exchanges containing approximately 5 grams of fat and 45 calories per serving include $1\frac{1}{2}$ tablespoons Nayonaise (tofu mayonnaise), 1 tablespoon tofu cream cheese, and 1 tablespoon coconut milk.

## VEGETARIAN FOODS THAT MAY BE NEW TO YOU

The vegetarian diet contains a wide variety of foods from which to choose. If you have recently become a vegetarian, see this as an opportunity to explore a whole new world of tastes and aromas. Here are some tips to get you started.

### Grains

Whole grains are good sources of fiber and vitamins, including vitamin E and some trace minerals. Refined grains are enriched with vitamins and minerals. This means that the hull, germ, and bran of the grain are removed and nutrients are then added back in. Some nutrients, as well as fiber, are lost during the refining process. It's better, particularly for people with diabetes, to choose whole grains as much as possible, due to their content of fiber and complex carbohydrates, which can help with control of blood sugar levels.

Once you start using brown rice, barley, quinoa, and the range of other grains available, you will enjoy more variety in the dishes you prepare with no extra work. When you cook grains, the measurement of water to grain does not need to be exact. Usually a dry grain will need a pot big enough to allow it to triple in volume. Two cups of water to one cup of grain is the basic proportion. (See Table 14 on page 46 for grain cooking information.)

Following is a list of some of the grains you can choose from. Many have found their way to shelves in most supermarkets, but natural food stores are still good places to find them.

## A Selected List of Whole Grains

*Amaranth*   Actually a seed, amaranth is used in cereal or ground into flour for bread. It is high in protein.

*Basmati rice*   A long-grain rice with a wonderful, nutty flavor, often used in Asian and Middle-Eastern cuisine.

*Brown rice*   Familiar to most Americans, brown rice is whole grain rice minus the outer husk. Because of the bran, it will take about 30 minutes longer to cook than white rice. It can be found as long, medium, or short grain rice.

*Buckwheat*   A seed which is used to make buckwheat flour, sometimes used to prepare pancakes. Buckwheat groats are the hulled, crushed kernels sold in coarse, medium, and fine grinds. It is native to Russia and is used to make kasha.

**Bulgur**   Wheat kernels that have been steamed, dried, and crushed. Bulgur is delicious prepared as a breakfast cereal with a little soymilk, or in pilafs or salads.

**Jasmine rice**   Fragrant rice similar to basmati, jasmine rice makes a wonderful, aromatic side dish or can be added to salads.

**Kamut**   A type of high-protein wheat mainly found in pastas, puffed cereals, and crackers. Kamut can be cooked and used in grain-based dishes and salads.

**Millet**   Rich in protein, this small, yellow, bland grain is used in cereals, pilafs, or is ground into flour for making bread.

**Pearled barley**   This popular type of barley adds great flavor and texture to breads, cereals, or soups. Whole-grain barley is also available.

## Table 14
## Cooking Chart for Grains

| Grain (1 cup) | Liquid (cups) | Cook Time (minutes) | Yield (cups) | Grain (1 cup) | Liquid (cups) | Cook Time (minutes) | Yield (cups) |
|---|---|---|---|---|---|---|---|
| Amaranth | 2½ | 20-25 | 2 | Kamut | 3 | 120 | 2¾ |
| Basmati rice | 2 | 50 | 2 | Millet | 3 | 30 | 3½ |
| Brown rice | 2 | 60 | 3 | Pearled barley | 3 | 60 | 3½ |
| Buckwheat | 2 | 15 | 2½ | Quinoa | 2 | 20 | 3½ |
| Bulgur | 2 | 15 | 2½ | Triticale | 3 | 120 | 2½ |
| Jasmine rice | 2 | 20 | 3 | Wheat berries | 3 | 135 | 2¼ |

*Quinoa*   A quick-cooking, high-protein grain, quinoa was a staple of the Incas. It can be used alone as a replacement for rice, or is delicious cooked with basmati rice.

*Triticale*    A nutty grain that is a hybrid of wheat and rye. Triticale contains more protein and less gluten than wheat. It can be found as whole berries, flakes, or flour and is good in cereals or grain dishes.

*Wheat berries*    An unprocessed whole grain that is delicious in salads, cereals, or baked into breads.

## Breads

When purchasing breads, be sure the label says "whole wheat flour" and not just "wheat flour." Wheat flour means the same as white flour in the commercial bread-baking world. According to the USDA federal standard, if bread is said to be "whole wheat," it must be 100% whole wheat.

Commercially baked bread may also contain more than a hundred food and chemical additives. Specialty breads, like rye, pumpernickel, corn, or other combinations, may contain more white flour than whole flours from which they were traditionally made. For example, pumpernickel, which was traditionally made from a combination of rye and whole wheat flours, may be mainly white flour with only a small percentage of rye flour and caramel coloring and molasses added to give it the appearance of pumpernickel.

If you cannot find a suitable whole wheat bread, buy flour and enjoy the satisfaction of baking your own. Whole wheat flour can be found in any supermarket. Keep it in the refrigerator or in a very cool place to avoid rancidity. You may also consider exploring the wide variety of flours made from other whole grains, which are available in supermarkets and natural food stores.

## Legumes

Legumes and grains are the primary sources of protein for vegetarians. Legumes are also rich sources of complex carbohydrates and iron. Below is a list of just some of the varieties that you can choose from and some suggestions for dishes in which to prepare them.

### A Selected List of Legumes

*Adzuki beans*    These small, reddish-brown beans make a great addition to soups, salads, or rice dishes.

*Black beans*    Black beans are best in soups, chili, and spicy dishes. Try mixing them with spicy salsa and corn and wrapping in a tortilla.

*Garbanzo beans*    Also called chick-peas, garbanzos compliment most grains. Add them to main dishes, salads, soups, and sandwiches. They are a tan, round-shaped bean, and take a longer time to cook than most beans except soy.

*Great northern beans and navy beans*    Most commonly used in "baked bean" recipes, these small, white beans are also delicious additions to soups.

*Kidney beans and pinto beans*    Often used interchangeably, kidney beans are red and kidney shaped. Pintos are beige with dark speckles. Both go well with all grains and are good in soups and casseroles.

*Lentils*    Tiny beans that look similar to split peas, lentils come in red, green, and brown. Lentils take only about 30 to 40 minutes to cook and are great in soups, casseroles, and stews.

*Lima beans*    A flat, white bean that is also sold as green lima beans that have been picked fresh and then frozen. Limas are good as a side dish or in soups or casseroles.

*Peanuts*    Although they are officially a legume, peanuts will be discussed under the section on nuts and seeds, as this is how they are most commonly used.

*Split peas*    Available in green or yellow, split peas are commonly used to make soup. You can also try serving them with a grain or as part of a casserole.

### Soyfoods

Derived from soybeans, these foods deserve a category of their own. Whole cooked soybeans can be used in many ways—soups, casseroles, salads, or puréed into a sandwich spread. Soybeans, like all other beans, must be cooked until they are completely soft. Most of the products that follow can be found in supermarkets or natural food stores.

**Tofu**, a versatile soybean product, is made from curdled soymilk that has been pressed into cakes. When processed with calcium sulfate, it is a rich source of calcium. Tofu has a smooth texture and mild flavor which blends well with any food. It needs no cooking, so it is great for fast meals, salads, and sandwiches. Both regular or low-fat tofu are available in silken, soft, firm, or extra-firm varieties. Enjoy firm or extra-firm tofu marinated, baked, added to stir-fry dishes, or scrambled. It can also be used as a substitute for eggs in baking. Use silken or soft tofu in salad dressings, dips, shakes, and pies.

**Tempeh** is a solid cake of fermented soybeans and grains resulting from a natural culturing process. It is low in calories and cholesterol-free. The flavor of tempeh depends on the combination of beans, grains, and nuts it is made from. Tempeh should be kept refrigerated or frozen and should be steamed for 10 minutes before using. It can be diced or grated and added to salads, sandwiches, soups, and casseroles. Marinating in herbs or spices and tamari can vary the flavor of tempeh. It can also be combined with cooked grains and vegetables.

**Textured soy protein** is made from defatted soy flour. The soy flour has had the oil extracted from it, and what remains is mostly protein and carbohydrate. It is then cooked under pressure and extruded and cut into pieces of various sizes. This dry, precooked food can then be rehydrated and made into many dishes. It is particularly compatible with tomato-based dishes such as chili or tomato sauce, but is also delicious in stroganoff and chicken-less noodle soup.

**Soy cheese and soy yogurts** are also available and make perfect substitutes for their milk-based counterparts. Be sure to check the ingredients when purchasing soy cheese. Some are made using dairy derivatives such as casein or whey.

**Soy flour** has a strong, nutty taste and can add complete protein to many recipes. Use it only in thoroughly cooked dishes or baked goods. Add ¼ cup per cup of whole wheat flour.

**Soy grits** are toasted pieces of the soybean. They can be added to casseroles or bread to replace chopped nuts, but with fewer calories and less fat.

**Miso** is a fermented, salty paste made from soybeans and other beans and grains. It comes in many colors and flavors. The sodium content varies but is less than salt. One teaspoon of sweet white miso has 140 to 290 mg of sodium (check the labels). Unpasteurized brands of miso contain valuable enzymes that can aid digestion. Miso can add flavor to many dishes. Try using a mixture of light and dark varieties. Miso should be kept refrigerated.

**Tamari** is a type of soy sauce. It is naturally aged and does not contain the chemical colorings that many soy sauces do. However, it is high in sodium and should be used sparingly.

## Nuts and Seeds

Nuts and seeds are as rich in protein as legumes, but they are also higher in calories and fat, particularly the unsaturated fats that have demonstrated many health benefits in current research. While nuts and seeds can add flavor and texture to many dishes, they should be used sparingly. (Dried sunflower seeds are 72% fat.)

Nuts are sold shelled or unshelled, except for cashews, which are never in a shell. If nuts are still in their shells, they are guarded against nutritional loss and chemical contamination. Unshelled nuts are treated with lye and gas to soften and loosen them from the shell. Nuts in the shell are usually bleached and may be colored or waxed. Use pistachios that haven't been dyed red. Inspect unshelled nuts to be sure they have no mold and a minimum of shell damage.

Nuts in the shell are unroasted, except for peanuts. Shelled nuts, however, may be raw or roasted and whole or in pieces. Almonds are blanched in a hot water bath to remove the outer skin, a process done for cosmetic reasons only. Unblanched almonds are also available and contain more nutrients.

Avoid buying nuts that have been roasted in oil and salt. They have additional fat roasted into them. Instead, go for unsalted, dry roasted nuts.

**Peanut butter** is probably the most well-known nut butter. However, a variety of other types are available on the market, such as almond or cashew butter. Try freshly ground nut butters or ones that are not highly processed. Be sure to store fresh nuts and nut butters in the refrigerator as they can go bad quickly.

You can, on occasion, try adding small amounts of nuts or seeds to main dishes, breakfast cereal, pancakes, baked products, salads, sandwiches, vegetable stir-fry dishes, and other dishes.

## Vegetables

Vegetables are excellent sources of complex carbohydrates, fiber, vitamins, and minerals, and generally contain very little calories and fat. Choose at least one dark green and one deep yellow or orange vegetable daily. All yellow, orange, and dark green vegetables, such as squash, carrots, and spinach, are good sources of vitamin A. Green leafy vegetables, such as collard greens, kale, and mustard greens, also supply vitamin C, iron, riboflavin, and calcium. When fresh, most vegetables are reliable sources of vitamin C, especially when eaten raw.

Choose fresh or frozen vegetables most often. Locally grown produce is a good choice. When purchasing fresh vegetables, be sure to wash them well. Scrub them in cold, soapy water. Soap can remove some chemicals that plain water cannot. Rinse them well. Select vegetables that look fresh and have no bruises. Handle them carefully and buy only what you need. Plan to eat them within one or two days. Root vegetables such as potatoes, carrots, parsnips, onions, and turnips can be kept longer, but they will also suffer some nutritional loss.

When cooking vegetables, try steaming. It is fast and helps to reduce the loss of nutrients. Steaming also helps to preserve the bright color of the vegetables. Broccoli retains its bright green and winter squash its bright orange. Steaming vegetables will also keep them flavorful.

Pressure-cooking is another excellent method. Timing must be accurate or the vegetables can quickly become overcooked. The greatest percentage of vitamins is retained using this method.

Cooking times for steaming or pressure-cooking varies from vegetable to vegetable. Experiment and cook until the vegetable is just tender, not mushy. When steaming vegetables, you will find that if you turn off the heat when they are half done, they will keep cooking if kept tightly covered. Frozen vegetables need little more than to be heated thoroughly by the steam, because they have already been blanched.

**Sea vegetables** are becoming increasingly popular because of their enormous nutritional value. They supply all of the 56 minerals and trace minerals your body requires. Sea veggies contain only 1% to 2% fat, mostly unsaturated. The most commonly used and readily available varieties are nori, dulse, kelp, and wakame. You'll find sea vegetables included in some of the recipes here.

## Fruits

Fruits, like vegetables, are abundant sources of complex carbohydrates, fiber, and a myriad of vitamins and minerals. They are generally low in fat and not too high in calories. When selecting, always look for those that are locally grown or in season. If you are concerned about herbicides or pesticides sprayed on fruits, try buying organic varieties instead.

When choosing fruit, pick ones that have a naturally good color, such as firm red or green apples with no bruises, preferably unwaxed. Bananas should be partially green and have few surface bruises. Wait until their jackets are a mellow yellow with a few brown speckles before eating; this is the peak of their ripeness. When buying berries, do not buy light colored ones (they are immature) or ones that are overripe; they should be plump and firm. When buying citrus, pick fruits that feel heavy for their size. Thin-skinned citrus are juicier. Avoid ones that yield to pressure (true of any fruit). Peaches, nectarines, and plums should be rich in color. Melons are often difficult fruits to judge for ripeness. Look for ones with even color and with a slight softening at the blossom end.

Fruits are rich in natural sugars, but manufacturers add sugar to some canned fruits to maintain the texture and as a preservative. It is possible to buy only lightly sweetened fruit or fruit preserved in its own juice. The label must state if sugar is added, so read the label.

Frozen fruits may have sugar added, especially berries. They may also have added colorings, salt, or acids. It is best to choose fresh seasonal fruits and limit the use of canned or frozen ones. Fruit juices generally contain very little or no fiber, so try to consume whole fruits as much as possible.

Dried fruits are concentrated sources of natural sugars, so be sure to consume them in small amounts. Sprinkle them on salads, cereal, or soy yogurt. Three prunes, $1\frac{1}{2}$ dried figs, or 2 tablespoons of raisins equal one fruit exchange, but they can be enjoyed in small amounts because their flavors are so concentrated. They can add a lot of flavor to a dish of oatmeal or a cup of soy yogurt.

When buying dried fruit, get sun-dried if possible. Avoid those with added sugar and preservatives.

### Nutritional Yeast

This food supplement comes in powder or flake form. It is not the same as brewer's yeast or baking yeast and can be used in yeast-free diets. All brands of nutritional yeast are high in B vitamins, but only Red Star Vegetarian Support Formula is fortified with $B_{12}$. This brand is particularly delicious with a slightly cheesy taste, and adds body and a deep flavor to sauces, gravies, soups, and spreads.

# COOKING AND SHOPPING TIPS

### Low-Fat Cooking

Learning to cook with less fat is an essential skill for people with type 2 diabetes. This does not necessarily mean less flavor.

There are many good brands of nonstick cookware available. Combined with a good nonstick oil spray, you can create dishes with great flavor and texture without a lot of oil. Lightly coating a nonstick pan can let you clarify onions, toast nuts and seeds, and create quick and tasty stir-fries.

You can also use your nonstick cookware to quickly cook vegetables in a little water with no oil. Just stir constantly and add small amounts of water as needed.

If you are converting a favorite recipe, there are a number of ways to reduce the fat content. Replacing meat with beans, grains, or vegan meat substitutes can help lower the fat content and eliminate saturated animal fat and cholesterol.

Skip the oil on your salad, and use only vinegar or lemon juice. Try out some low-calorie, no-fat dressings to find one you like.

## Shopping Tips

➤ Take advantage of the "free" foods (no calories) allowed in the diabetic diet. Just a few raw vegetables, such as cucumbers and celery, eaten with lunch and dinner can help satisfy your appetite while adding vitamins, minerals, and fiber to your diet.

➤ Experiment with different herbs to help eliminate any salt cravings. Try replacing your salt shaker with a combination of your favorite herbs and sea vegetables, or try some of the commercial mixes.

➤ "Dietetic" on a label does not mean "diabetic." Those foods are reduced in calories, but may still not be freely used. Read the labels.

➤ Buy sugar-free tomato sauce or make your own.

➤ If you buy fruit juice, read the labels and buy only 100% juice. If it is called "fruit juice" on the label, it must be 100% real fruit juice. Products labeled "fruit drinks" and "fruit-flavored drinks" have lots of water, sugar, and flavorings.

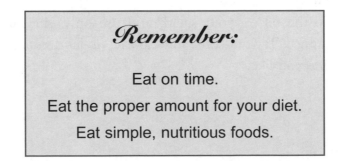

## *Remember:*

Eat on time.

Eat the proper amount for your diet.

Eat simple, nutritious foods.

# MENU PLANNING

| 1,500 CALORIE MEAL PLAN |
|---|
| 2 low-fat soymilk    9 starch    3 fruit    4 vegetable    3 meat    4 fat |

| DAY 1 | DAY 2 | DAY 3 | DAY 4 | DAY 5 |
|---|---|---|---|---|
| **Breakfast**<br>2 Oatmeal Pancakes (p. 63) 1 tsp. soy margarine | **Breakfast**<br>Figgy Brown Rice Cereal (p. 66) with 6 almonds ¾ cup low-fat soymilk | **Breakfast**<br>Banana-Raisin Bran Biscuit (p. 76) with 1 teaspoon soy margarine 1 cup low-fat soymilk | **Breakfast**<br>English Muffin (p. 75) 2 teaspoons cashew butter ¾ cup fruit flavored soy yogurt | **Breakfast**<br>Hot Oatmeal (p. 69) with 1 cup low-fat soymilk |
| **Snack**<br>1 slice bread with 1 ounce soy cheese | **Snack**<br>apple | **Snack**<br>Blueberry Smoothie Delight (p. 71) | **Snack**<br>3 ounce grapes | **Snack**<br>½ cup calcium-fortified juice |
| **Lunch**<br>2 servings Tabouli (p. 87) 1 ounce seitan orange | **Lunch**<br>1 cup salad greens with 1 cup raw vegetables and Three Bean Delight (p. 89) ½ cup calcium-fortified juice 2 Herbed Wheat Rolls (p. 77) | **Lunch**<br>½ whole wheat pita with Falafel (p. 131) tahini dressing, alfalfa sprouts, and chopped tomatoes steamed broccoli 2 plums | **Lunch**<br>Black Bean Vegetable Soup (p. 108) apple | **Lunch**<br>Split Pea Soup (p. 110) carrot sticks 1 cup honey-dew melon with lemon |
| **Snack**<br>1 small banana with 4 chopped walnut halves | **Snack**<br>Orange Cranberry Muffin (p. 80) | **Snack**<br>¾ ounce pretzels | **Snack**<br>1 serving whole wheat crackers with 2 tsp. nut butter | **Snack**<br>2 Apple-Oat Drop Cookies (p. 150) |
| **Dinner**<br>Meatless Loaf (p. 129) Steamed spinach and mushrooms Baked Diced Potatoes (p. 142) 1 tsp soy margarine 1 cup low-fat soy milk | **Dinner**<br>1 Soft Taco (p. 122) with ¼ avocado ⅔ cup brown rice steamed zucchini and peppers 1 cup low-fat soymilk | **Dinner**<br>Meaty Mushroom Pilaf (p. 125) Small salad with sunflower seeds and One-calorie Herb Dressing (p. 96) 1 cup low-fat soy milk | **Dinner**<br>Broccoli Rice Casserole (p. 118) 1 Herbed Wheat Roll (p. 77) 1 tsp. soy margarine steamed carrots 1 cup low-fat soy milk | **Dinner**<br>2 pieces Breaded Baked Tofu (p. 115) ⅔ cup Millet and shi-itake (p.121) asparagus cooked with 1 tsp. canola oil 1 cup low-fat soy milk |

# 2,000 CALORIE MEAL PLAN

2 low-fat soymilk    13 starch    4 fruit    4 vegetable    4 meat    5 fat

| DAY 1 | DAY 2 | DAY 3 | DAY 4 | DAY 5 |
|---|---|---|---|---|
| **Breakfast**<br>Mushroom Scrambled Tofu (p. 67)<br>3 slices Basic Whole Wheat Bread (p. 74) with 2 tsp. soy margarine | **Breakfast**<br>4 Whole Buckwheat Pancakes (p. 62)<br>1¼ cup strawberries<br>2 tsp. soy margarine and ½ cup low-fat soy milk | **Breakfast**<br>Bulgur Wheat Hot Cereal (p. 68) with 1 medium banana<br>¾ cup low-fat soy milk<br>2 slices Basic Whole Wheat Bread (p. 74) with 2 Tbsp. almond butter | **Breakfast**<br>Figgy Brown Rice Cereal (p. 66)<br>¾ cup fruit flavored soy yogurt<br>3 Tbsp. wheat germ | **Breakfast**<br>Tofu French Toast (p. 65)<br>1 tsp. margarine<br>¾ cup low-fat soy milk<br>½ cup fresh fruit |
| **Snack**<br>Banana Smoothie (p. 70) | **Snack**<br>The Best English Muffin (p. 75)<br>1 ounce soy cheese | **Snack**<br>Raisin Tofu Scone with 1 tsp. margarine | **Snack**<br>Blueberry Muffin (p. 82) | **Snack**<br>½ bagel with 2 tsp. nut butter<br>½ cup calcium-fortified juice |
| **Lunch**<br>Southwest Sandwich (p. 101)<br>1 cup raw vegetables and 2 Tbsp. Yogurt Herb Dip (p. 93) and ½ pear | **Lunch**<br>Easy Lentil Stew (p. 107)<br>Steamed spinach<br>Whole grain crackers (2 servings)<br>1 cup cantaloupe | **Lunch**<br>Tofu Pita Pizzas (p. 104)<br>Kale Potato Soup (p. 109) | **Lunch**<br>2 servings Quick Tofu Salad (p. 90) with 2 Tbsp. Lemon-Tomato Juice Dressing (p. 95) and 1 whole wheat pita<br>1 cup Swiss chard with soy sauce and 1 tsp. sesame oil | **Lunch**<br>2 servings Yeasty Vegetable Crepes (p. 64)<br>small salad with "Russian" Yogurt Dressing (p. 94)<br>Herbed Wheat Roll (p. 77)<br>apple |
| **Snack**<br>Popcorn (p. 152) | **Snack**<br>Blueberry Smoothie (p. 71) made with rice milk | **Snack**<br>Fruit smoothie made with ½ cup soy yogurt and ½ papaya | **Snack**<br>Five-Fruit salad (p. 148) | **Snack**<br>2 rice cakes |
| **Dinner**<br>Miso Soup (p. 110)<br>¼ cup tofu with 1 tsp. oil<br>⅔ cup brown rice steamed kale and mushrooms | **Dinner**<br>2 servings Oriental Tofu (p. 120) with 1 Tbsp. sesame seeds<br>1 Sesame-Cornmeal Biscuit (p. 79) with 1 tsp. soy margarine<br>½ cup mango | **Dinner**<br>1½ servings Vegetable Fried Rice (p. 117) | **Dinner**<br>Lighter Side of BLTs (p. 103)<br>2 cups vegetable soup<br>carrot and celery sticks | **Dinner**<br>1½ cups pasta with ½ cup Cheezy Bechamel Sauce (p. 144)<br>broccoli and mushrooms sauteed in 1½ tsp. oil |
| **Snack**<br>1 cup low-fat soy milk<br>¾ cup bran cereal<br>¾ cup blueberries | **Snack**<br>Quick rice pudding (p. 151) | **Snack**<br>3 cups popcorn with 1 tsp. soy margarine | **Snack**<br>1 cup low-fat soy milk<br>1 cup corn flakes<br>4 walnut halves | **Snack**<br>½ cup low-fat soy milk<br>¾ ounce pretzels<br>orange |

*Breakfast*

# Buckwheat Pancakes

Yield: 12 pancakes

*Pancakes are a great way to kick off the day. You can easily make them to suit your own taste or use whatever ingredients you have on hand.*

Mix together in a medium bowl:

¾ cup buckwheat flour
¾ cup whole wheat flour
1½ teaspoons baking powder
½ teaspoon sugar or granulated sweetener of choice
¼ teaspoon salt

Beat in:

2 cups low-fat soymilk
1 teaspoon oil
1 teaspoon vanilla

Lightly spray a nonstick frying pan with oil on medium-high. When the pan is hot, drop on the batter ¼ cup at a time. Flip once when bubbles appear, and cook until golden brown on the bottom, about 1 to 2 minutes on each side. Spray as necessary to prevent sticking.

*Variations: Drop a few fresh or frozen blueberries or strawberries in the batter. Save some for topping to give them that special touch. You can also try topping the pancakes with a little all-fruit spread.*

| Per Serving (2 pancakes): Exchanges | |
|---|---|
| ⅓ milk, 1⅓ starch | |
| Calories | 149 |
| Total Fat | 2 g |
| % of calories from fat | 12% |
| Saturated Fat | 1 g |
| Protein | 5 g |
| Carbohydrate | 27 g |
| Fiber | 4 g |
| Sodium | 203 mg |
| Calcium | 97 mg |

# Oatmeal Pancakes

Yield: 8 pancakes

*These pancakes go great with peanut butter. A little fruit in the batter or as a topping will give them extra sweetness and flavor.*

Mix together in a medium bowl:

1½ cups rolled oats
½ cup whole wheat flour
2 teaspoons baking powder
1 teaspoon cinnamon

Beat in:

1¼ cups low-fat soymilk
1 tablespoon oil
¼ cup raisins

Lightly spray a nonstick frying pan with oil on medium-high. When the pan is hot, drop on the batter by tablespoons. Flip once when bubbles appear, and cook until golden brown on the bottom. Spray the pan as necessary to prevent sticking.

| Per Serving (2 pancakes): Exchanges | |
|---|---|
| 1 bread, ½ fruit, ½ milk | |
| Calories | 263 |
| Total Fat | 6 g |
| % of calories from fat | 20% |
| Saturated Fat | 1 g |
| Protein | 8 g |
| Carbohydrate | 45 g |
| Fiber | 6 g |
| Sodium | 26 mg |
| Calcium | 31 mg |

# Yeasty Vegetable Crepes

Yield: 10 crepes (5 servings)

*These adaptable griddle treats have spinach and red peppers for color and crunch, but you can use whatever vegetables you have on hand.*

In a mixing bowl combine:

> ¾ cup finely ground whole wheat flour
> ¾ cup nutritional yeast flakes
> ½ teaspoon salt
> 1 teaspoon minced garlic

Stir in:

> ½ cup chopped spinach
> ¼ cup chopped red bell pepper
> ¼ cup chopped sweet onion
> 1 tablespoon oil

Pour in and mix:

> 1½ cups water

Coat a nonstick frying pan with olive oil spray over medium heat. When the pan is hot, pour in about ¼ cup of the batter. Spread it out if needed with a spoon to make it an even thickness. Cook until lightly browned on one side, flip, and cook until lightly browned on the other side. Serve with low-sodium salsa, hot peanut sauce, or ketchup. Try chopped fresh tomatoes or sliced mushrooms in the batter.

| Per Serving: (2 crepes) Exchanges | |
|---|---|
| 1 meat, 1 starch, ⅓ vegetable | |
| Calories | 148 |
| Total Fat | 4 g |
| % of calories from fat | 24% |
| Saturated Fat | 1 g |
| Protein | 13 g |
| Carbohydrate | 21 g |
| Fiber | 3 g |
| Sodium | 224 mg |
| Calcium | 141 mg |

# Tofu French Toast

Yield: 6 pieces of toast

*If you love French toast, here's a recipe worth trying.*
*These have no cholesterol and not much fat but great taste.*

Mix in a blender until smooth:

  ½ pound tofu
  ¾ cup low-fat soymilk
  2 tablespoons brown sugar
  ½ teaspoon cinnamon

Pour the blended mixture into a shallow dish. Dip
into the mixture:

  6 slices whole wheat bread

Cook on a nonstick pan lightly sprayed with
cooking oil until just brown on both sides.

| Per Serving (2 pieces): Exchanges | |
|---|---|
| 2⅓ starch, ⅔ meat | |
| Calories | 242 |
| Total Fat | 8 g |
| % of calories from fat | 29% |
| Saturated Fat | 1 g |
| Protein | 11 g |
| Carbohydrate | 34 g |
| Fiber | 5 g |
| Sodium | 236 mg |
| Calcium | 133 mg |

# Figgy Brown Rice Cereal

Yield: 1 serving

*Brown rice can be the basis for a delicious breakfast treat.*
*Figs add sweetness here, as well as increase the calcium.*

Bring to a boil in a small saucepan:

> ⅔ cup water
> ⅓ cup brown rice

Cover and simmer for 30 minutes. Remove from the heat.

Add:

> 2 figs, chopped
> ¼ teaspoon nutmeg

Serve in a bowl with:

> ¼ cup low-fat soymilk or soy yogurt

| Per Serving: | |
|---|---|
| **Exchanges** | |
| 2 bread, 1 fruit, 1 milk | |
| Calories | 349 |
| Total Fat | 3 g |
| % of calories from fat | 7% |
| Saturated Fat | 1 g |
| Protein | 7 g |
| Carbohydrate | 76 g |
| Fiber | 8 g |
| Sodium | 32 mg |
| Calcium | 83 mg |

# Mushroom-Scrambled Tofu

Yield: 2 servings

*This quick-to-fix, high-protein meal will get you through the morning with energy to spare.*

Lightly coat a nonstick pan with cooking oil over medium heat. Sauté for 2 minutes:

> 1 small onion, sliced
> ½ cup sliced mushrooms
> ½ cup chopped red bell pepper

Stir and add a little water if necessary to keep from sticking. Add and scramble until heated through:

> ½ pound tofu, crumbled
> 2 tablespoons nutritional yeast flakes
> 1 teaspoon soy sauce
> ¼ teaspoon curry powder
> 1 tablespoon finely chopped cilantro
> (optional)

*Variations:* Serve with salsa on the side.

*For a flavor variation, leave out the soy sauce and try adding a half teaspoon of chick-pea miso that has been dissolved in a tablespoon of warm water. You can use shiitake mushrooms if you like.*

| Per Serving: | |
|---|---|
| **Exchanges** | |
| 1 meat, 1 vegetable | |
| Calories | 145 |
| Total Fat | 6 g |
| % of calories from fat | 37% |
| Saturated Fat | 1 g |
| Protein | 15 g |
| Carbohydrate | 13 g |
| Fiber | 3 g |
| Sodium | 179 mg |
| Calcium | 188 mg |

# Bulgur Wheat Hot Cereal

Yield: 1 serving

*Bulgur is a great choice for a hot breakfast in a hurry. A medium or fine grind bulgur will cook up quick with a chewy texture and a nutty flavor.*

Bring to a boil in a small saucepan:

⅔ cup water
⅓ cup bulgur wheat

Cover and simmer until the liquid is absorbed.

Process to a fine powder in a blender:

2 tablespoons cashews

Add and blend again:

½ teaspoon vanilla
¼ cup low-fat soymilk or soy yogurt

Pour over the bulgur and cook for 5 more minutes. Add:

1 banana, sliced

| Per Serving: | |
|---|---|
| **Exchanges** | |
| 2½ bread, 1 fruit, 2 fat, 1 milk | |
| Calories | 395 |
| Total Fat | 10 g |
| % of calories from fat | 22% |
| Saturated Fat | 2 g |
| Protein | 11 g |
| Carbohydrate | 72 g |
| Fiber | 12 g |
| Sodium | 31 mg |
| Calcium | 40 mg |

# *Hot Oatmeal*

Yield: 1 serving

*Oatmeal has always been a morning standard. It's fast, healthful, and you can flavor it however you like. Try this combination for a delicious start to your day.*

Mix in a small pan:

> 1 cup hot water
> ⅔ cup rolled oats

Cook gently for 5 to 6 minutes.

Add:

> 1 tablespoon raisins
> ½ teaspoon cinnamon
> 1 tablespoon sunflower seeds

Serve with:

> ¼ cup low-fat soymilk or soy yogurt

| Per Serving: | |
|---|---|
| **Exchanges** | |
| 2 bread, 1 fruit, 1 fat, 1 milk | |
| Calories | 316 |
| Total Fat | 9 g |
| % of calories from fat | 25% |
| Saturated Fat | 1 g |
| Protein | 12 g |
| Carbohydrate | 50 g |
| Fiber | 8 g |
| Sodium | 22 mg |
| Calcium | 47 mg |

# Banana Smoothie

Yield: 1 serving

*This is a good use for bananas that have been sitting around and may have turned a little brown. You can also keep a supply of frozen bananas on hand. Just peel and chop some ripe bananas, and place in freezer bags in the freezer. They will be ready to thicken up your smoothie any time you want.*

Combine in a blender until smooth and creamy:

1 cup low-fat soymilk
1 teaspoon vanilla
1 frozen banana
Pinch of cinnamon or nutmeg
2 ice cubes (optional)

*Variations: Try adding some other fruits like blueberries, peaches, strawberries, pineapple, or whatever strikes your fancy.*

| Per Serving: | |
|---|---|
| **Exchanges** | |
| 1½ milk, 2 fruit | |
| Calories | 225 |
| Total Fat | 3 g |
| % of calories from fat | 12% |
| Saturated Fat | 1 g |
| Protein | 5 g |
| Carbohydrate | 48 g |
| Fiber | 5 g |
| Sodium | 71 mg |
| Calcium | 31 mg |

# Blueberry Smoothie Delight

Yield: 1 cup

*Fresh or frozen blueberries give this smoothie an irresistible taste.
The addition of a little soymilk powder provides extra protein
and makes a thicker smoothie.*

Blend together until smooth:

    ½ cup blueberries
    ½ cup low-fat vanilla soymilk, rice milk*, or other dairy-free milk
    ⅓ frozen banana
    1 teaspoon vanilla
    1 ice cube
    1 tablespoon soymilk powder (optional)

*\*If you use rice milk, the exchange will be
1 fruit, 1 starch.*

| Per Serving: | |
|---|---|
| **Exchanges** | |
| 1 fruit, 1 milk | |
| Calories | 135 |
| Total Fat | 1 g |
| % of calories from fat | 6% |
| Saturated Fat | 0 g |
| Protein | 3 g |
| Carbohydrate | 30 g |
| Fiber | 4 g |
| Sodium | 40 mg |
| Calcium | 19 mg |

# Golden Gravy

Yield: 3½ cups

*Use this versatile sauce on steamed or raw vegetables, potatoes, grains, or biscuits.*

Have all your ingredients ready and the milk warm before you start. Sauté in a nonstick pan lightly sprayed with oil until the onions are clear:

  1 cup chopped onions
  1 cup chopped shiitake mushrooms

Set the onion-mushroom mixture aside. In a heavy-bottomed saucepan, stir constantly with a whisk over medium heat until lightly brown:

  ½ cup whole wheat pastry flour

Add while stirring:

  2 tablespoons olive oil

Slowly add while continuing to stir:

  1½ cups warm low-fat soymilk
  ½ cup warm water

As the gravy begins to thicken, add:

  the onion-mushroom mixture
  ¾ cup nutritional yeast flakes
  2 tablespoons mellow red miso

| Per Half Cup: | |
|---|---|
| **Exchanges** | |
| 1 starch, 1 meat, 1 fat | |
| Calories | 147 |
| Total Fat | 5 g |
| % of calories from fat | 29% |
| Saturated Fat | 0 g |
| Protein | 10 g |
| Carbohydrate | 19 g |
| Fiber | 3 g |
| Sodium | 241 mg |
| Calcium | 55 mg |

Continue stirring and thin with warm water to the desired consistency. The gravy should be fairly thick before adding the miso, which will thin the gravy considerably. Do not boil once the miso has been added. Beat out any lumps with the whisk. Serve over whole grain toast or biscuits.

# Breads

# Basic Whole Wheat Bread

Yield: 1 loaf (8 servings)

*A little bit of maple syrup in a yeast bread makes the bread rise better. One tablespoon in a loaf of bread does not contribute significant calories. The bread can be made without it, but if you are new to working with whole wheat, you may find that you need help in getting it to rise. A little maple syrup may be all you need.*

Stir together in a large bowl until the yeast is dissolved:

> 1 tablespoon maple syrup
> 1 tablespoon baking yeast
> 2½ cups warm water

Beat in:

> 1½ cups whole wheat flour

Mix in gradually:

> 1½ cups additional whole wheat flour

On a lightly floured surface, knead the dough until it is soft and springy. Form into two loaves and place in two lightly oiled 9 x 5-inch bread pans. Cover the pans with a clean towel. Let the bread rise until almost double in size. Preheat the oven to 350°F. Bake the bread for 45 minutes. For bread machines, follow the instructions for adding the wet and dry ingredients, and adjust the ingredient amounts if needed.

| Per Serving: | |
|---|---|
| **Exchanges** | |
| 2 bread | |
| Calories | 161 |
| Total Fat | 1 g |
| % of calories from fat | 5% |
| Saturated Fat | 0 g |
| Protein | 6 g |
| Carbohydrate | 35 g |
| Fiber | 6 g |
| Sodium | 3 mg |
| Calcium | 18 mg |

# The Best English Muffins

Yield: 12 (4-inch) muffins

*In case you haven't heard, English muffins aren't just for breakfast any more. You can split and cover them with your own pasta sauce to make little pizzas, or wrap them around a slice of baked tofu for a delightfully different sandwich.*

Combine and set aside:

> 2 tablespoons baking yeast
> ½ cup whole wheat pastry flour

Heat in a small saucepan until warm:

> 1¾ cups low-fat soymilk
> 1 tablespoon liquid sweetener (optional)
> 2 tablespoons oil

Stir the yeast and flour into the milk mixture, and combine until dissolved. Pour this into a large bowl.

Beat in:

> 4 cups whole wheat pastry or
>    unbleached flour

Preheat the oven to 350°F.

Knead the dough for ten minutes on a lightly floured surface. Roll out the dough and cut into twelve 4-inch rounds. Place the rounds on a floured baking sheet.

Let the rounds rise in a warm place for 1 hour, then bake for about 25 minutes.

| Per Muffin: | |
|---|---:|
| **Exchanges** | |
| 2 bread, 1 fat | |
| Calories | 194 |
| Total Fat | 3 g |
| % of calories from fat | 13% |
| Saturated Fat | 1 g |
| Protein | 7 g |
| Carbohydrate | 36 g |
| Fiber | 6 g |
| Sodium | 13 mg |
| Calcium | 18 mg |

# Banana-Raisin Bran Biscuits

Yield: 12 biscuits

*The fruit gives these biscuits a slightly sweet flavor.*

Preheat the oven to 350°F.

Combine in a medium mixing bowl:

> 1½ cups whole wheat pastry flour
> ½ cup wheat bran
> 2 teaspoons baking powder

Stir in:

> ½ cup low-fat soymilk
> 1 teaspoon vanilla
> 1 banana, mashed

Add:

> ½ cup raisins
> ½ cup chopped walnuts

Drop onto an ungreased cookie sheet, making 12 biscuits. Bake for 15 minutes.

| Per Biscuit: | |
|---|---|
| **Exchanges** | |
| 1 bread, 1 fruit | |
| Calories | 129 |
| Total Fat | 4 g |
| % of calories from fat | 27% |
| Saturated Fat | 1 g |
| Protein | 4 g |
| Carbohydrate | 21 g |
| Fiber | 4 g |
| Sodium | 5 mg |
| Calcium | 8 mg |

# Herbed Wheat Rolls

Yield: 10 rolls

*These little buns are great for accompanying a salad or a vegetable soup.*

Preheat the oven to 350°F.

Heat in a small saucepan until warm:

>    1 cup low-fat soymilk

Add:

>    1 tablespoon baking yeast
>    2 teaspoons canola oil

Beat in:

>    1½ cups whole wheat flour
>    ½ teaspoon dill
>    ½ teaspoon oregano
>    ½ teaspoon thyme

Drop by tablespoons onto a floured baking sheet, making 10 rolls. Bake for about 15 minutes.

| Per Roll: | |
|---|---|
| **Exchanges** | |
| 1 bread | |
| Calories | 83 |
| Total Fat | 1 g |
| % of calories from fat | 11% |
| Saturated Fat | 1 g |
| Protein | 3 g |
| Carbohydrate | 15 g |
| Fiber | 3 g |
| Sodium | 8 mg |
| Calcium | 9 mg |

# Raisin Tofu Scones

Yield: 10 scones

*The raisins give these little pastries sweetness and flavor and give you an energy boost as well.*

Preheat the oven to 350°F.

Sift together:

> 2 cups whole wheat pastry flour
> 2 teaspoons baking powder

Add:

> ½ pound tofu, mashed
> 1 cup low-fat soymilk
> 2 tablespoons liquid sweetener
> 1 teaspoon vanilla
> ½ cup raisins

Mix all the ingredients well. Roll out on a floured surface. Cut into 10 triangles and place on an ungreased baking sheet. Bake for 15 minutes.

| Per Scone: | |
|---|---|
| **Exchanges** | |
| 1 bread, 1 fruit | |
| Calories | 135 |
| Total Fat | 1 g |
| % of calories from fat | 6% |
| Saturated Fat | 0 g |
| Protein | 4 g |
| Carbohydrate | 29 g |
| Fiber | 4 g |
| Sodium | 11 mg |
| Calcium | 21 mg |

# Sesame-Cornmeal Biscuits

Yield: 12 biscuits

*Sesame seeds are a good source of calcium,*
*and give added interest to these biscuits.*

Preheat the oven to 350°F.

Mix together thoroughly in a medium mixing bowl:

> 1 cup whole wheat pastry flour
> ⅔ cup cornmeal
> ⅓ cup wheat germ
> 2 teaspoons baking powder
> 1 tablespoon sesame seeds

Add and beat well:

> 1 tablespoon oil
> 1 cup low-fat soymilk

Drop onto a floured cookie sheet by table-spoons, making 12 biscuits. Bake 20 to 25 minutes.

| Per Biscuit: | |
|---|---|
| **Exchanges** | |
| 1 bread, ½ fat | |
| Calories | 100 |
| Total Fat | 3 g |
| % of calories from fat | 27% |
| Saturated Fat | 1 g |
| Protein | 3 g |
| Carbohydrate | 16 g |
| Fiber | 3 g |
| Sodium | 9 mg |
| Calcium | 11 mg |

# Orange Cranberry Muffins

Yield: 12 muffins

*Dried cranberries give these muffins a unique flavor.*

Preheat the oven to 350°F.

Mix together in a medium bowl:

> 1½ cups whole wheat pastry flour
> ½ cup oats, coarsely ground in a blender
> ½ tablespoon baking powder
> ½ tablespoon baking soda
> ½ teaspoon cinnamon

Blend together:

> ¾ cup orange juice
> ½ tablespoon vanilla
> ¼ cup unsweetened applesauce
> ¾ cup crumbled tofu

Add carefully to the dry ingredients, and avoid overmixing.

Fold in:

> ½ cup dried cranberries

Bake in lightly oiled or nonstick muffin cups for 20 to 25 minutes.

Raisins can be substituted for the cranberries.

| Per Serving: | |
|---|---|
| **Exchanges** | |
| 1 bread | |
| Calories | 85 |
| Total Fat | 1 g |
| % of calories from fat | 10% |
| Saturated Fat | 0 g |
| Protein | 4 g |
| Carbohydrate | 16 g |
| Fiber | 2 g |
| Sodium | 2 mg |
| Calcium | 21 mg |

# Strawberry Muffins

Yield: 12 muffins

*These muffins make a colorful addition to your breakfast table.*

Preheat the oven to 350°F.

Mix together in a medium bowl:

> 1 cup whole wheat pastry flour
> 1 cup oats, coarsely ground in a blender
> ½ teaspoon cinnamon
> 2 teaspoons baking powder

Blend together:

> 1 tablespoon liquid sweetener
> ¼ cup low-fat soymilk or rice milk
> ¾ pound tofu, crumbled
> 3 tablespoons unsweetened
>    applesauce
> 1 teaspoon vanilla

Add carefully to the dry ingredients, and avoid overmixing.

Fold in:

> ½ cup sliced strawberries

Bake in lightly oiled or nonstick muffin cups for 20 to 25 minutes.

| Per Serving: | |
|---|---|
| **Exchanges** | |
| 1 starch | |
| Calories | 99 |
| Total Fat | 2 g |
| % of calories from fat | 18% |
| Saturated Fat | 0 g |
| Protein | 5 g |
| Carbohydrate | 15 g |
| Fiber | 3 g |
| Sodium | 4 mg |
| Calcium | 35 mg |

# Blueberry Muffins

Yield: 12 muffins

*Everybody's favorite muffins, light and delicious, without the eggs and with a lot less fat. Ground flaxseed replaces the eggs in this recipe.*

In a bowl mix:

> 2 cups whole wheat pastry flour
> 2 teaspoons baking powder
> Pinch of salt
> ½ cup sugar

In a separate bowl combine:

> 1 cup low-fat soymilk
> 3 tablespoons oil
> 1 teaspoon vanilla

Preheat the oven to 350°F. Finely chop in a coffee or spice grinder:

> 2 teaspoons flaxseeds

Mix with:

> 4 tablespoons warm water

| Per Muffin: | |
|---|---|
| **Exchanges** | |
| 1⅔ starch, 1 fat | |
| Calories | 155 |
| Total Fat | 4 g |
| % of calories from fat | 23% |
| Saturated Fat | 1 g |
| Protein | 3 g |
| Carbohydrate | 26 g |
| Fiber | 2 g |
| Sodium | 7 mg |
| Calcium | 4 mg |

Let stand for a minute, then add to the liquid ingredients. Stir the liquid ingredients into the dry ingredients, and lightly mix. Some lumps are fine. Stir in:

> 1 cup fresh or frozen blueberries

Spoon into lightly oiled muffin tins. Bake for 20 to 25 minutes until light brown around the edges. Let cool for 10 minutes before removing from the muffin tins.

# Salads and Dressings

# Basic Free Green Salad

Enjoy up to 2 cups free!

  2 cups shredded romaine lettuce
  2 cups shredded iceberg lettuce
  1 cup curly endive
  1 cup shredded spinach or Swiss chard
  12 sliced or whole radishes
  1 cucumber, sliced
  2 stalks celery, diced, with tops

Other ingredients to form your own combinations:

  Boston or bibb lettuce
  Shredded red or green cabbage
  Kale or comfrey
  Chicory or sorrel
  Lamb's-quarters leaves
  Parsley or watercress
  Turnip, collard, mustard, dandelion,
      or beet greens
  Green or wax beans
  Onions
  Tomatoes
  Sprouts
  Sliced fresh mushrooms
  Sliced fresh red or green peppers
  Florets of broccoli or cauliflower
  Slices of zucchini or yellow squash
  Brussels sprouts, halved or quartered
  Scallions or chives

| Per Serving: | |
|---|---|
| **Exchanges** | |
| 1 vegetable | |
| Calories | 30 |
| Total Fat | 1 g |
| % of calories from fat | 0% |
| Saturated Fat | 1 g |
| Protein | 2 g |
| Carbohydrate | 6 g |
| Fiber | 3 g |
| Sodium | 53 mg |
| Calcium | 76 mg |

# Garbanzo-Noodle Salad with Miso Ginger Sauce

Yield: 4 servings

Mix together:

> 1 cup cooked garbanzos
> 2 cups cooked whole wheat noodles
> 2 tablespoons finely chopped red onions (optional)
> 1 cup chopped broccoli, steamed until just tender
> 1 cup chopped carrots, steamed until just tender
> ½ cup chopped red bell pepper
> 2 tablespoons chopped fresh parsley
> ¼ teaspoon garlic powder

To make the sauce, grind in a blender until fine:

> 1 tablespoon cashews

Add and blend until smooth:

> ½ cup plain soymilk or rice milk
> 1 tablespoon miso
> 1 tablespoon grated fresh ginger
> 1 teaspoon low-sodium soy sauce
> 1 tablespoon cornstarch

Heat the sauce over medium heat, and let it bubble for 15 seconds. Remove from the heat and mix with the noodles and vegetables. Chill and serve.

| Per Serving: | |
|---|---|
| **Exchanges** | |
| 1 meat, 1 starch, 1 vegetable | |
| Calories | 139 |
| Total Fat | 3 g |
| % of calories from fat | 19% |
| Saturated Fat | 0 g |
| Protein | 7 g |
| Carbohydrate | 23 g |
| Fiber | 5 g |
| Sodium | 245 mg |
| Calcium | 52 mg |

# Fat-Free Carrot Salad

Yield: 2 servings

*Here's a quick any-time salad with great crunch, a little sweetness, and the zest of citrus.*

Mix together:

> 1 cup grated carrots
> ½ apple, grated
> ¼ cup raisins

Pour over and mix thoroughly:

> 2 tablespoons orange juice
> 1 teaspoon lemon juice

Refrigerate for at least half a day.

| Per Serving: | |
|---|---|
| **Exchanges** | |
| 1 vegetable, 1½ fruit | |
| Calories | 98 |
| Total Fat | 0 g |
| % of calories from fat | 0% |
| Saturated Fat | 0 g |
| Protein | 1 g |
| Carbohydrate | 25 g |
| Fiber | 4 g |
| Sodium | 24 mg |
| Calcium | 23 mg |

# Tabouli

Yield: 8 servings

*With the addition of some chick-peas, this hearty Lebanese salad can make a full meal.*

Bring to a boil:

    4 cups water

Add:

    2 cups bulgur wheat

Remove from the heat and set aside for 30 minutes.

Put the cooked bulgur into a salad bowl, and mix in the rest of the ingredients:

    2 cups chopped tomatoes
    2 tablespoons olive oil
    2 cloves garlic, minced
    3 tablespoons chopped chives
    ½ cup chopped parsley
    1 tablespoon lemon juice
    Salt and pepper to taste

Refrigerate overnight.

| Per Serving: | |
|---|---|
| **Exchanges** | |
| 1½ bread, 1 vegetable, ½ fat | |
| Calories | 155 |
| Total Fat | 4 g |
| % of calories from fat | 23% |
| Saturated Fat | 1 g |
| Protein | 5 g |
| Carbohydrate | 28 g |
| Fiber | 7 g |
| Sodium | 13 mg |
| Calcium | 23 mg |

# Rice Salad

Yield: 6 servings

*This is a hearty salad that works well for lunch, potlucks, picnics, or a roadside meal when traveling.*

Combine all the ingredients and mix well:

2 cups cooked brown rice
½ cup finely chopped onion
½ cup finely chopped celery
½ cup grated carrot
½ cup broccoli or alfalfa sprouts
1 cup cooked kidney beans
1 cup finely chopped tomato
1 teaspoon olive oil
½ tablespoon apple cider vinegar
¼ teaspoon salt
½ tablespoon mixed herbs, such as basil, parsley, garlic powder, oregano, thyme etc.

Serve warm or refrigerate and serve cold.

| Per Serving: | |
|---|---|
| **Exchanges** | |
| 1⅓ starch, ⅓ meat, 1 vegetable | |
| Calories | 134 |
| Total Fat | 2 g |
| % of calories from fat | 13% |
| Saturated Fat | 0 g |
| Protein | 5 g |
| Carbohydrate | 26 g |
| Fiber | 4 g |
| Sodium | 108 mg |
| Calcium | 26 mg |

# Three-Bean Delight

Yield: 4 servings

*If you use rinsed canned beans, this couldn't be easier to make!*

Toss together:

> 1 cup cooked kidney beans
> 1 cup cooked garbanzo beans
> 1 cup cooked lima beans
> 1 cup chopped onion
> ½ cup chopped green bell pepper
> 4 teaspoons olive oil

Serve hot or cold with a grain or bread. To serve cold for a salad, add a few drops of lemon juice or vinegar.

| Per Serving: | |
|---|---|
| **Exchanges** | |
| 2½ meat, 1 fat | |
| Calories | 238 |
| Total Fat | 6 g |
| % of calories from fat | 22% |
| Saturated Fat | 1 g |
| Protein | 12 g |
| Carbohydrate | 36 g |
| Fiber | 10 g |
| Sodium | 7 mg |
| Calcium | 55 mg |

# Quick Tofu Salad

Yield: 4 servings

*When you're in a hurry and need some protein,*
*here's a quick and tasty combination.*

Mix together:

> 1 pound tofu, diced
> ½ cup chopped tomatoes
> ¼ cup chopped peppers and onions

Place on a bed of lettuce, and garnish with:

> ¼ cup sliced cucumbers
> ¼ cup sprouts

Use Lemon-Tomato Juice Dressing
(page 95) or your favorite fat-free dressing.

| Per Serving (no dressing): Exchanges | |
|---|---|
| 1 meat, 2 fat, 2 vegetable | |
| Calories | 178 |
| Total Fat | 10 g |
| % of calories from fat | 51% |
| Saturated Fat | 1 g |
| Protein | 19 g |
| Carbohydrate | 8 g |
| Fiber | 4 g |
| Sodium | 19 mg |
| Calcium | 245 mg |

# Tofu Salad Spread

Yield: 4 servings

*This tofu spread is good on bread, crackers, stuffed into pitas, etc.*
*It's easy to mix up and makes a great picnic sandwich.*

Mix in a large bowl, and chill:

  1 pound tofu, crumbled
  ½ cup diced sweet onions
  ¼ cup diced red bell peppers
  ¼ cup grated carrots (optional)
  ¼ cup diced dill pickles
  ¼ cup diced sweet pickles or sweet pickle relish
  ¼ cup nutritional yeast flakes
  2 tablespoons soy mayonnaise
  1 teaspoon tamari (optional)

| Per Serving: | |
|---|---|
| **Exchanges** | |
| 1 meat, 1 starch | |
| Calories | 160 |
| Total Fat | 7 g |
| % of calories from fat | 39% |
| Saturated Fat | 1 g |
| Protein | 14 g |
| Carbohydrate | 13 g |
| Fiber | 2 g |
| Sodium | 451 mg |
| Calcium | 179 mg |

# Tofu Potato Salad

Yield: 2 servings

*This full-bodied salad makes a satisfying hot weather dish.*

Steam:

> 1 cup diced potatoes

Mix together in a medium bowl with the diced potatoes:

> ⅓ (12.3-ounce) package low-fat, firm silken tofu, crumbled
> ½ cup diced tomatoes
> 1 green onion, chopped
> ½ cup chopped bell pepper
> ¼ cup chopped celery
> 1 tablespoon chopped fresh parsley
> 1 teaspoon tarragon
> ½ teaspoon oregano
> ¼ teaspoon basil
> 1 tablespoon sunflower seeds
> 1 teaspoon soy mayonnaise

Serve warm or chilled.

| Per Serving: | |
|---|---|
| **Exchanges** | |
| 3 meats, 2 breads, 2 fats, 1 vegetable | |
| Calories | 309 |
| Total Fat | 8 g |
| % of calories from fat | 23% |
| Saturated Fat | 1 g |
| Protein | 15 g |
| Carbohydrate | 49 g |
| Fiber | 8 g |
| Sodium | 956 mg |
| Calcium | 98 mg |

# *Yogurt Herb Dressing*

Yield: 1 cup

*This makes a nice dip for crackers and raw veggies too.*

Mix together thoroughly:

 1 cup soy yogurt
 4 tablespoons chives
 1 teaspoon tarragon
 1 teaspoon dill
 ½ teaspoon basil
 ½ teaspoon marjoram
 1 tablespoon lemon juice

| **Per 2 tablespoons:** | |
|:---|---:|
| **Exchanges** | |
| 1 tablespoon free | |
| Calories | 11 |
| Total Fat | 1 g |
| % of calories from fat | 81% |
| Saturated Fat | 1 g |
| Protein | 1 g |
| Carbohydrate | 1 g |
| Fiber | 1 g |
| Sodium | 4 mg |
| Calcium | 3 mg |

# "Russian" Yogurt Dressing

Yield: 1½ cups

*All kinds of salad greens are good for you, and this dressing makes them even more appealing!*

Mix together thoroughly:

> 2 tablespoons sugar-free ketchup
> 1 cup soy yogurt
> ¼ cup water
> 1 clove garlic, minced
> 2 tablespoons chopped dill pickle
> 2 tablespoons chopped chives
> ½ teaspoon mustard powder
> ½ teaspoon tamari

| **Per 2 tablespoons:** | |
|---|---|
| **Exchanges** | |
| 1 tablespoon free | |
| Calories | 8 |
| Total Fat | 0 g |
| % of calories from fat | 0% |
| Saturated Fat | 0 g |
| Protein | 1 g |
| Carbohydrate | 1 g |
| Fiber | 1 g |
| Sodium | 44 mg |
| Calcium | 1 mg |

# Lemon-Tomato Juice Dressing

Yield: 1⅓ cups

*This dressing is perfect for the Quick Tofu Salad on page 90.*

Mix together thoroughly:

> 1 cup tomato juice
> 2 tablespoons lemon juice
> 1 teaspoon basil
> 2 tablespoons chopped onion
> 1 tablespoon chopped parsley

| Per 2 tablespoons: | |
|---|---|
| **Exchanges** | |
| 1 to 3 tablespoons free | |
| Calories | 6 |
| Total Fat | 0 g |
| % of calories from fat | 0% |
| Saturated Fat | 0 g |
| Protein | 1 g |
| Carbohydrate | 1 g |
| Fiber | 0 g |
| Sodium | 88 mg |
| Calcium | 3 mg |

# One-Calorie Herb Dressing

Yield: 1 cup

*Here's a tasty way to take advantage of the tremendous health benefits of apple cider vinegar.*

Mix together thoroughly:

> ½ cup apple cider or wine vinegar
> ½ cup water
> 1 teaspoon celery seed
> 1 teaspoon dill seed
> ½ teaspoon dry mustard
> ½ teaspoon pepper

| Per 2 tablespoons: | |
|---|---|
| **Exchanges** | |
| 1 tablespoon free | |
| Calories | 2 |
| Total Fat | 0 g |
| % of calories from fat | 0% |
| Saturated Fat | 0 g |
| Protein | 0 g |
| Carbohydrate | 1 g |
| Fiber | 0 g |
| Sodium | 0 mg |
| Calcium | 3 mg |

# Miso Dressing

Yield: ¾ cup

*This easy, fat-free dressing can be used on any green salad.*

Combine in a blender:

    1 clove garlic, chopped
    1 tablespoon strawberry or raspberry all-fruit preserves
    2 tablespoons apple cider vinegar
    1 tablespoon sweet white miso
    ⅔ cup water

| Per 2 tablespoons: | |
|---|---|
| **Exchanges** | |
| free food | |
| Calories | 14 |
| Total Fat | 0 g |
| % of calories from fat | 0% |
| Saturated Fat | 0 g |
| Protein | 1 g |
| Carbohydrate | 3 g |
| Fiber | 0 g |
| Sodium | 105 mg |
| Calcium | 3 mg |

# Herb Mix

Yield: 1½ cups

*Use this free food herb mix as a seasoning for soups, stews, and other dishes, including Baked Tofu (page 114), Tofu Shepherd's Pie (page 127), and Cheezy Bechamel Sauce (page 144).*

Combine ¼ cup each of these dried herbs:

Oregano
Tarragon
Parsley
Garlic powder
Basil
Savory

Place the herbs in a glass jar, and stir. Add 1 or 2 teaspoons salt if desired. Keep the jar closed in a dark, cool place.

# Sandwiches and Soups

# Ratatouille Pitas

Yield: 1 serving

*Ratatouille is a traditional French dish which features two of the less commonly used vegetables, eggplant and zucchini. Stuffing this mixture into a pita pocket makes it easy and fun to eat and keeps the serving size small.*

Preheat the oven to 325°F.

Simmer in a medium saucepan until tender:

> 1 tablespoon chopped onion
> ½ cup diced tomato
> ½ cup diced zucchini or eggplant
> 2 tablespoons water

Remove from the heat.

Mix in:

> ¼ cup grated soy cheddar cheese
> 1 tablespoon nutritional yeast flakes

Slice open:

> 1 (2-ounce) whole wheat pita bread

Fill the pita bread with the vegetable mixture. Wrap in foil and heat in the oven until thoroughly warm, about 5 minutes.

Spread on top:

> ¼ cup alfalfa sprouts

| Per Serving: | |
|---|---|
| **Exchanges** | |
| 2 meat, 2 starch, 1 vegetable | |
| Calories | 258 |
| Total Fat | 7 g |
| % of calories from fat | 24% |
| Saturated Fat | 1 g |
| Protein | 19 g |
| Carbohydrate | 34 g |
| Fiber | 7 g |
| Sodium | 513 mg |
| Calcium | 95 mg |

# Southwest Sandwich

Yield: 1 serving each

*Here's a flavorful combination that's high in protein.*

Mix together and spread on 2 slices of whole wheat bread:

¼ cup mashed cooked pinto beans
2 teaspoons tomato sauce
1 teaspoon chopped onion
2 tablespoons grated soy cheddar cheese
Shredded lettuce

| Per Serving: (with 2 slices whole wheat bread) Exchanges 1 meat, 1 starch | |
| --- | --- |
| Calories | 174 |
| Total Fat | 3 g |
| % of calories from fat | 14% |
| Saturated Fat | 1 g |
| Protein | 11 g |
| Carbohydrate | 29 g |
| Fiber | 4 g |
| Sodium | 308 mg |
| Calcium | 47 mg |

# Middle Eastern Sandwich

Yield: 1 serving

*Garbanzo beans and sesame tahini are the basis of the popular dip, hummus. Here they combine with sprouts and tomatoes for a tasty lunch treat.*

Mix together and spread on 2 slices whole wheat bread:

¼ cup mashed cooked garbanzo beans
2 teaspoons tahini
1 teaspoon chopped onion
Pinch of garlic powder
1 teaspoon lemon juice
¼ cup chopped tomatoes
¼ cup sprouts

| Per Serving: (with 2 slices whole wheat bread) Exchanges | |
|---|---|
| 1½ meat, ½ fat | |
| Calories | 211 |
| Total Fat | 7 g |
| % of calories from fat | 29% |
| Saturated Fat | 1 g |
| Protein | 9 g |
| Carbohydrate | 132 g |
| Fiber | 6 g |
| Sodium | 262 mg |
| Calcium | 87 mg |

# Lighter Side Of BLTs

Yield: 1 serving

*Here's a quick version of a favorite sandwich. There are several varieties of great-tasting, low-fat bacon substitutes that have no animal products. Try them out and find the ones you like for different dishes. This BLT has almost 100 fewer calories, one-fifth the fat, and 4 times the fiber of a regular white-bread BLT.*

2 slices whole wheat bread, toasted
2 teaspoons soy mayonnaise
4 slices veggie Canadian bacon
2 slices tomato
1 leaf romaine lettuce

You can just pile on the toppings or, if you prefer a crisper "bacon," you can heat up the veggie slices for a minute in a nonstick pan lightly sprayed with oil.

| Per Serving: | |
|---|---|
| **Exchanges** | |
| 2 starch, 3 meat | |
| Calories | 269 |
| Total Fat | 5 g |
| % of calories from fat | 16% |
| Saturated Fat | 1 g |
| Protein | 0 g |
| Carbohydrate | 30 g |
| Fiber | 6 g |
| Sodium | 984 mg |
| Calcium | 9 mg |

# Tofu Pita Pizzas

Yield: 1 serving

*Low-calorie pita bread is the perfect ready-made
crust for these pizza snacks.*

Preheat the oven to 325°F.

Separate into two halves and place on a baking sheet:

　　1 (2-ounce) pita bread

Mix together and place on the pita halves:

　　½ (12.3-ounce) package low-fat, firm silken tofu, diced
　　½ cup chopped mushrooms
　　4 thin slices onion
　　4 thin slices green bell pepper
　　2 tablespoons tomato sauce

Top with:

　　2 tablespoons soy Parmesan

Bake for 10 to 15 minutes.

| Per Serving: | |
|---|---|
| **Exchanges** | |
| 2 starch, 2 meat, 1 vegetable | |
| Calories | 275 |
| Total Fat | 5 g |
| % of calories from fat | 16% |
| Saturated Fat | 1 g |
| Protein | 27 g |
| Carbohydrate | 34 g |
| Fiber | 7 g |
| Sodium | 914 mg |
| Calcium | 227 mg |

# Tortilla Wraps

Yield: 2 wraps

*Wraps are adaptable, fun to make, and can be made to suit any taste.*
*Look for different types of tortillas to use for your wraps.*
*Here is a basic idea to get you started.*

Have ready:

> 2 8-inch whole wheat tortillas

Prepare:

> ½ small cucumber, peeled and sliced into thin strips
> ½ cup grated carrots
> 1 tomato, thinly sliced
> ¼ cup sprouts
> ¼ red bell pepper, sliced into thin strips
> ½ cup shredded lettuce
> 4 ounces marinated tofu, thinly sliced

Spread each tortilla with half of:

> 1 tablespoon soy mayonnaise
> 1 teaspoon mustard (optional)

Divide the rest of the ingredients evenly and place on the tortillas. Roll and enjoy.

| Per Serving: (1 wrap) Exchanges | |
|---|---|
| 1 starch, 1 vegetable | |
| Calories | 176 |
| Total Fat | 5 g |
| % of calories from fat | 25% |
| Saturated Fat | 1 g |
| Protein | 9 g |
| Carbohydrate | 30 g |
| Fiber | 5 g |
| Sodium | 252 mg |
| Calcium | 106 mg |

# Creamy Garbanzo Soup

Yield: 4 servings

*This combination of vegetables cooks up into a soup that is as colorful as it is flavorful.*

Soak overnight in 8 cups water:

  1½ cups garbanzo beans

Drain the beans. Cook the soaked beans until soft (about 2 hours) with:

  2 cups chopped onion
  ½ cup chopped celery
  ½ cup diced carrots
  6 cups water

Puree in a blender, then return to the pot.

Stir in:

  2 cups low-fat soymilk
  ¼ cup soymilk powder

Steam and add to the soup:

  1½ cups diced carrots

Season to taste with:

  Pepper
  Parsley
  Kelp (see page 54)

| Per Serving: | |
|---|---|
| **Exchanges** | |
| 2 meat, 2 starch, 1 vegetable | |
| Calories | 221 |
| Total Fat | 3 g |
| % of calories from fat | 12% |
| Saturated Fat | 0 g |
| Protein | 10 g |
| Carbohydrate | 39 g |
| Fiber | 8 g |
| Sodium | 73 mg |
| Calcium | 76 mg |

# Easy Lentil Stew

Yield: 6 servings

*Lentils are small brown beans that give this stew a full body and dark color.*

Cook for about 1 hour:

>    1 cup dry lentils
>    1 cup brown rice
>    Thyme, oregano, and pepper to taste
>    6 cups water

Add more water if needed.

Add and cook another 15 minutes:

>    2 cups diced carrots
>    1 cup chopped onions
>    2 stalks celery with tops, diced
>    1 medium tomato, chopped
>    1 cup shredded spinach (optional)

| Per Serving: | |
|---|---|
| **Exchanges** | |
| ½ meat, 2½ starch, 1 vegetable | |
| Calories | 220 |
| Total Fat | 1 g |
| % of calories from fat | 4% |
| Saturated Fat | 0 g |
| Protein | 11 g |
| Carbohydrate | 43 g |
| Fiber | 10 g |
| Sodium | 33 mg |
| Calcium | 46 mg |

# Black Bean Vegetable Soup

Yield: 2 servings

*One of the keys to a good, healthy diet is learning to make a good bean soup. Experiment with different types of beans and different recipes until you find the ones you really enjoy. Packed with protein, fiber, vitamins, and very little fat, bean soups can be one of the dishes that become part of your regular meal plan.*

Have ready:

> ½ cup cooked black beans

Bring to a boil in a 2-quart saucepan, cover, and simmer for 10 minutes:

> ½ cup fresh or frozen corn
> ½ cup fresh or frozen green beans
> ½ cup diced carrots
> ½ cup diced celery
> 1 cup shredded spinach or cabbage
> ¼ cup chopped onions
> 2 cups water
> ½ teaspoon each: parsley,
> oregano, basil

Add:

> 1 teaspoon tomato sauce
> the cooked beans
> ¼ cup whole wheat or enriched
> noodles

Simmer until the noodles are cooked.

| Per Serving: | |
|---|---|
| **Exchanges** | |
| 2 starch, 1½ vegetable, ½ meat | |
| Calories | 190 |
| Total Fat | 1 g |
| % of calories from fat | 4% |
| Saturated Fat | 0 g |
| Protein | 10 g |
| Carbohydrate | 40 g |
| Fiber | 10 g |
| Sodium | 83 mg |
| Calcium | 84 mg |

# Kale Potato Soup

Yield: 6 servings

*Kale is a wonder vegetable, rich in antioxidants, phytochemicals, and calcium, all of which help your body's metabolism to work better. This is an easy, delicious way to take advantage of the benefits of kale.*

Bring to a boil and cook until the potatoes are soft:

> 5 cups water
> 1 large onion, chopped
> 2 cloves garlic, minced
> 3 medium potatoes, chopped
> Salt and pepper to taste

Add:

> 4 cups chopped kale, steamed

Remove half the soup and process in a blender. Return the blended mixture to the pot, and stir. Serve hot.

| Per Serving: | |
|---|---|
| **Exchanges** | |
| 1 vegetable, 1 bread | |
| Calories | 93 |
| Total Fat | 0 g |
| % of calories from fat | 0% |
| Saturated Fat | 0 g |
| Protein | 3 g |
| Carbohydrate | 21 g |
| Fiber | 3 g |
| Sodium | 23 mg |
| Calcium | 72 mg |

# *Miso Soup*

Yield: 3 servings

*Miso soup is simple and delicious. You can add some tofu for protein, spinach or kale for vitamins, and a few green onions for taste, and have a nutritious, satisfying soup in no time. If you keep the soup from boiling after you add the miso, you can preserve all of the miso's nutritional value. Nori, a popular sea vegetable, is a traditional and delicious addition. (See pages 51 and 54.)*

Heat to almost boiling:

    3 cups water

Add and simmer for 10 minutes:

    ¼ pound tofu, cubed
    ½ cup chopped fresh spinach
    ½ cup sliced shiitake mushrooms
    1 green onion, chopped

Remove from the heat. Stir in until dissolved:

    3 tablespoons mellow white miso

Sprinkle on top:

    2 tablespoons finely chopped
        toasted nori (optional)

| Per Serving: | |
|---|---|
| **Exchanges** | |
| 1 starch | |
| Calories | 81 |
| Total Fat | 3 g |
|   % of calories from fat | 33% |
|   Saturated Fat | 0 g |
| Protein | 6 g |
| Carbohydrate | 10 g |
| Fiber | 2 g |
| Sodium | 422 mg |
| Calcium | 53 mg |

# Split Pea Soup

Yield: 4 (1½-cup) servings

*This thick, creamy soup, packed with vegetables, is almost a meal in itself.*

Cook covered for 1 hour:

> 1 cup dried split peas
> ¼ cup uncooked barley
> 6 cups water

Add:

> 1 cup diced potato
> 1 cup chopped onions
> 1 cup shredded cabbage
> 1 stalk celery, diced
> 1 cup diced carrots
> Bay leaf, basil, tarragon,
> and pepper to taste

Cover and cook another 30 minutes.

| Per Serving: | |
|---|---|
| **Exchanges** | |
| 1 meat, 1 vegetable, 2½ starch | |
| Calories | 212 |
| Total Fat | 1 g |
| % of calories from fat | 2% |
| Saturated Fat | 0 g |
| Protein | 12 g |
| Carbohydrate | 42 g |
| Fiber | 14 g |
| Sodium | 27 mg |
| Calcium | 49 mg |

# Tofu Vegetable Soup

Yield: 2 servings

*You can throw together leftover vegetables that you may have lying around for any number of variations on this basic soup.*

Cook for 15 minutes:

> 2 tablespoons uncooked brown rice
> 2 cups water

Add and simmer for 10 to 15 minutes longer:

> ¾ cup sliced carrots
> 1 small potato, diced
> ¼ cup fresh or frozen peas
> ½ cup sliced celery
> ½ cup chopped onions
> Tarragon, bay leaf, basil, celery seed to taste

Stir in:

> ½ pound firm tofu, cut into bite-sized pieces

| Per Serving: | |
|---|---|
| **Exchanges** | |
| 2 starch, 1 meat, 2 vegetable | |
| Calories | 157 |
| Total Fat | 3 g |
| % of calories from fat | 17% |
| Saturated Fat | 1 g |
| Protein | 8 g |
| Carbohydrate | 26 g |
| Fiber | 5 g |
| Sodium | 40 mg |
| Calcium | 94 mg |

*Main Dishes*

# *Baked Tofu*

Yield: 3 servings

*This dish is a staple in vegetarian diets. It's good as a stand-alone snack, or as the protein part of a complete meal. You can even slip it between two slices of bread for a tasty and hearty sandwich.*

Have ready:

>1 pound firm tofu, sliced

Marinate the tofu for 1 hour in:

>3 tablespoons tamari
>2 tablespoons finely chopped onion
>1 tablespoon Herb Mix (page 98)
>1 tablespoon canola oil

Bake on a cookie sheet for 20 minutes at 375°F.

After 10 minutes, turn the tofu over and sprinkle with:

>Fresh chives

| Per Serving: | |
|---|---|
| **Exchanges** | |
| 1½ meat, 1 fat | |
| Calories | 170 |
| Total Fat | 12 g |
| % of calories from fat | 63% |
| Saturated Fat | 1 g |
| Protein | 14 g |
| Carbohydrate | 4 g |
| Fiber | 2 g |
| Sodium | 106 mg |
| Calcium | 164 mg |

# Breaded Baked Tofu

Yield: 9 pieces

*You can eat these hot right out of the oven or refrigerate them and serve cold on sandwiches with your favorite condiments.*

Preheat the oven to 350°F. Cut into 9 slices:

> 1 pound firm tofu

In a bowl, place:

> 2 tablespoons tamari

In a separate bowl, mix:

> 3 tablespoons whole wheat flour
> 3 tablespoons nutritional yeast flakes
> ¼ teaspoon garlic powder

Dip each piece of tofu in the tamari. Let the excess drip off, and coat with the flour and yeast mixture.

Place on a cookie sheet that has been lightly oiled with 1 teaspoon oil. There will be tamari and flour mixture left over.

Bake for 20 minutes, flip the tofu, and bake for 15 more minutes.

| Per Piece: | |
|---|---|
| **Exchanges** | |
| 1 meat | |
| Calories | 50 |
| Total Fat | 3 g |
| % of calories from fat | 50% |
| Saturated Fat | 0 g |
| Protein | 5 g |
| Carbohydrate | 2 g |
| Fiber | 1 g |
| Sodium | 116 mg |
| Calcium | 7 mg |

# *Grainburgers*

Yield: 8 burgers

*Here's a good way to use up any leftover brown rice you may have.*

Mix:

>    2 cups cooked brown rice
>    ⅓ cup cornmeal
>    ⅓ cup whole wheat flour
>    ⅓ cup oatmeal
>    2 tablespoons dried parsley
>    1 teaspoon turmeric
>    1 teaspoon garlic powder
>    ½ teaspoon salt

Simmer in ½ cup water for 10 minutes:

>    ⅓ cup chopped celery
>    ⅓ cup chopped onion

Mix the celery and onion into the dry ingredients along with:

>    ½ cup mashed tofu

Form eight patties and brown each side in a nonstick skillet.

| Per Burger: | |
|---|---|
| **Exchanges** | |
| 1 starch | |
| Calories | 116 |
| Total Fat | 1 g |
| % of calories from fat | 8% |
| Saturated Fat | 0 g |
| Protein | 4 g |
| Carbohydrate | 22 g |
| Fiber | 3 g |
| Sodium | 149 mg |
| Calcium | 17 mg |

# Vegetable Fried Rice

Yield: 4 servings

*It's easy to cook up crisp vegetables with little or no added fat. If you like your vegetables softer, just add a little water, cover, and steam for a minute or two.*

Simmer for 45 minutes until the liquid is absorbed:

> ½ cup brown rice
> 1½ cups water

Cut into strips or dice, steam for 10 minutes, and cool:

> 8 ounces tempeh

In a well-seasoned wok or nonstick pan, brown the tempeh, lightly spraying with cooking oil and adding a little water if necessary to keep from sticking. Stir while cooking to brown all sides.

Stir in:

> ¼ cup sliced onions
> ½ cup sliced celery
> ½ cup sliced carrots
> ¼ cup diced red bell pepper
> ¼ cup chopped spinach leaves

Sauté a few minutes, then add the cooked rice. Mix all the ingredients together, and add:

> 1 tablespoon tamari

Sprinkle on top to serve:

> ¼ cup chopped green onions

| Per Serving: | |
|---|---|
| **Exchanges** | |
| 1 meat, 1 starch, 1 vegetable | |
| Calories | 218 |
| Total Fat | 5 g |
| % of calories from fat | 21% |
| Saturated Fat | 1 g |
| Protein | 14 g |
| Carbohydrate | 32 g |
| Fiber | 6 g |
| Sodium | 288 mg |
| Calcium | 10 mg |

# Broccoli Rice Casserole

Yield: 4 servings

*This is a favorite vegetable dish for a family dinner or a potluck.*

Crumble into a small pan, and toast:

> 2 slices whole wheat bread
> 1 teaspoon oil

Set aside.

Simmer together over low heat for 45 minutes:

> 1 cup uncooked brown rice
> 3 cups water
> ¼ teaspoon each: pepper, basil, and tarragon
> ½ teaspoon oregano
> ½ teaspoon kelp powder
> ½ cup chopped onion

Mix in:

> 1 (12.3-ounce) package low-fat, firm tofu, mashed
> 2 tablespoons nutritional yeast flakes
> 1 (10-ounce) package frozen chopped broccoli, cooked

Place the mixture in an ungreased 8 x 8-inch casserole dish, and top with:

> 4 ounces soy cheese, grated
> the toasted bread crumbs

Heat in the oven for a few minutes to melt the cheese.

| Per Serving: | |
|---|---|
| **Exchanges** | |
| 2 starch, 2 meat | |
| Calories | 270 |
| Total Fat | 9 g |
| % of calories from fat | 31% |
| Saturated Fat | 1 g |
| Protein | 19 g |
| Carbohydrate | 28 g |
| Fiber | 5 g |
| Sodium | 352 mg |
| Calcium | 106 mg |

# Millet & Broccoli

Yield: 2 servings

*Here's a savory grain and vegetable combination that's spiced up with the addition of nori, a highly nutritious sea vegetable. (See page 54.)*

Simmer over low heat until the liquid is absorbed:

½ cup uncooked millet
1¼ cups water
½ cup chopped onions

Mix into the cooked millet:

¼ cup diced red bell pepper
2 tablespoons finely chopped nori
2 teaspoons tamari
2 teaspoons balsamic vinegar
¼ teaspoon salt (optional)

Serve warm or cold.

| Per Serving: | |
|---|---|
| **Exchanges** | |
| 3 starch | |
| Calories | 319 |
| Total Fat | 10 g |
| % of calories from fat | 28% |
| Saturated Fat | 2 g |
| Protein | 12 g |
| Carbohydrate | 46 g |
| Fiber | 8 g |
| Sodium | 9 mg |
| Calcium | 205 mg |

# *Oriental Tofu*

Yield: 2 servings

*You can add water chestnuts or snow peas to this basic recipe for a dish that tastes even more like it comes from your local Chinese restaurant.*

Simmer for 5 minutes:

    1 cup sliced or halved mushrooms
    ½ cup sliced onions
    ½ cup water

Add and cook about 35 minutes or more until the rice is tender:

    ⅓ cup uncooked brown rice
    ⅓ cup water
    1 teaspoon tamari

Add and cook another 5 minutes:

    ¾ cup diced firm tofu (6 ounces)

| Per Serving: | |
|---|---|
| **Exchanges** | |
| 1 meat, 1 vegetable, 2 starch | |
| Calories | 232 |
| Total Fat | 5 g |
| % of calories from fat | 19% |
| Saturated Fat | 1 g |
| Protein | 12 g |
| Carbohydrate | 36 g |
| Fiber | 5 g |
| Sodium | 181 mg |
| Calcium | 112 mg |

# Millet & Shiitake

Yield: 2 servings

*If you like a lighter grain, try this recipe with quinoa instead of the millet.*

Soak in hot water for 10 minutes:

¼ cup dried shiitake mushrooms

Chop the soaked mushrooms.

Cover and simmer over low heat until the liquid is absorbed (about 25 minutes):

½ cup uncooked millet
1¼ cups water
½ cup chopped onion
the soaked mushrooms

Mix into the cooked millet:

¼ cup diced red bell pepper

Mix and stir into the millet:

2 tablespoons mellow white miso
2 tablespoons water

Stir in:

2 teaspoons chopped walnuts
½ cup chopped, steamed broccoli

Serve warm or cold.

| Per Serving: | |
|---|---|
| **Exchanges** | |
| 3 starch, 1 vegetable, 1 fat | |
| Calories | 338 |
| Total Fat | 7 g |
| % of calories from fat | 20% |
| Saturated Fat | 1 g |
| Protein | 12 g |
| Carbohydrate | 58 g |
| Fiber | 6 g |
| Sodium | 422 mg |
| Calcium | 30 mg |

# Soft Tacos

Yield: 8 tacos

*You can save yourself the fat and cholesterol of fast food places and whip up these Tex Mex wraps at home.*

Preheat the oven to 350°F.

> 2 cups mashed cooked pinto beans
> 8 corn tortillas

Heat the beans. Place ¼ cup in each tortilla, fold, and place upright in a baking dish.

In a small saucepan, combine and cook slowly until thick:

> ¼ cup salsa
> 2 tablespoons soy yogurt
> 1 tablespoon unbleached flour

Pour the sauce over the tortillas, and heat in the oven for 10 minutes.

| Per Taco: | |
|---|---|
| **Exchanges** | |
| 2 starch | |
| Calories | 171 |
| Total Fat | 1 g |
| % of calories from fat | 5% |
| Saturated Fat | 0 g |
| Protein | 7 g |
| Carbohydrate | 33 g |
| Fiber | 6 g |
| Sodium | 66 mg |
| Calcium | 51 mg |

# Stir-Fry Vegetable Tofu

Yield: 2 servings

*Stir-frying can be a great way to create a quick, colorful meal. With a well seasoned wok or good nonstick pan, you can do it with little or no oil. You can use an oil spray, but use it sparingly.*

Have all of your vegetables and spices ready. Heat a nonstick skillet on high, and lightly spray with oil. Add:

> ½ pound tofu, cubed
> 2 cups fresh or frozen chopped vegetables
> (any combination of these: celery, bell peppers, onion, peas, carrots, broccoli, or any other favorite vegetables)
> 1 tablespoon grated fresh ginger

Add the hardest vegetables first, and cook over medium-high heat, stirring to prevent sticking. Add a little water if the vegetables begin to stick.

Mix and stir into the cooked vegetables:

> 2 tablespoons miso
> 1 tablespoon mirin

*Note: Mirin is a Japanese sweet sake (rice wine) often used in cooking to temper the salty flavor of miso.*

| Per Serving: | |
|---|---|
| **Exchanges** | |
| 1 meat, 1 vegetable, 1 fat | |
| Calories | 185 |
| Total Fat | 8 g |
| % of calories from fat | 41% |
| Saturated Fat | 1 g |
| Protein | 14 g |
| Carbohydrate | 9 g |
| Fiber | 4 g |
| Sodium | 526 mg |
| Calcium | 27 mg |

# Soy Burgers

Yield: 3 servings

*There are a variety of vegetarian "burger" products on the market, but you can save money by making your own at home. Adjust the seasonings to your own taste.*

Mash:

> 1 cup cooked soybeans

Mix with:

> 2 tablespoons nutritional yeast flakes
> 1 cup quick-cooking rolled oats
> 1 tablespoon tamari

Preheat the oven to 350°F.

Sauté:

> ¼ cup chopped onion
> 1 clove garlic, minced
> ½ teaspoon oregano
> ½ teaspoon basil
> 1 tablespoon oil

Add to the beans. Mix well and form 6 flat patties. Bake on a lightly oiled cookie sheet for 10 minutes.

Turn the burgers over and top with:

> ¼ cup tomato sauce

Bake 10 to 15 minutes more.

| Per Serving: | |
|---|---|
| **Exchanges** | |
| 1 meat, 1 fat, 2⅓ starch | |
| Calories | 275 |
| Total Fat | 12 g |
| % of calories from fat | 39% |
| Saturated Fat | 1 g |
| Protein | 18 g |
| Carbohydrate | 28 g |
| Fiber | 7 g |
| Sodium | 462 mg |
| Calcium | 115 mg |

# "Meaty" Mushroom Pilaf

Yield: 4 servings

*Textured soy protein granules are an excellent substitute for ground beef in almost any recipe. They are especially good when combined with mushrooms, as in this dish.*

Have ready and warmed:

>   3 cups cooked brown rice
>   1½ cups cooked textured soy protein granules (See page 50.)

Simmer until the greens are tender:

>   2 cups chopped mushrooms
>   1 cup chopped kale or spinach
>   ¼ cup chopped onions
>   2 tablespoons parsley
>   2 teaspoons oil
>   ¼ cup water

Stir in the rice and textured soy protein until well combined.

| Per Serving: | |
|---|---|
| **Exchanges** | |
| 1 vegetable, 1 meat, 2 starch | |
| Calories | 253 |
| Total Fat | 4 g |
| % of calories from fat | 14% |
| Saturated Fat | 1 g |
| Protein | 13 g |
| Carbohydrate | 42 g |
| Fiber | 5 g |
| Sodium | 25 mg |
| Calcium | 74 mg |

# Tempeh & Mushroom Stuffing

Yield: 1 serving

*Here is a quick and delicious tempeh recipe that can be easily doubled to make extra servings.*

Preheat the oven to 350°F.

Simmer together:

> 2 tablespoons tomato sauce
> ½ cup chopped mushrooms
> ¼ cup chopped onions
> 1 clove garlic, minced
> Dash of black pepper
> 2 tablespoons water

Remove from heat and mix in until hot:

> 2 slices whole wheat bread, crumbled
> 2 tablespoons soy Parmesan cheese

Slice in half and steam for 10 minutes:

> 4 ounces tempeh

Lay the tempeh in a dish, and pour the vegetable mixture over it. Cover and bake for 15 minutes.

| Per Serving: | |
|---|---|
| **Exchanges** | |
| 3 starch, 4 meat | |
| Calories | 408 |
| Total Fat | 25 g |
| % of calories from fat | 30% |
| Saturated Fat | 2 g |
| Protein | 33 g |
| Carbohydrate | 47 g |
| Fiber | 12 g |
| Sodium | 649 mg |
| Calcium | 233 mg |

# Tofu Shepherd's Pie

Yield: 4 servings

*This is another good dish for a potluck.*

Wash and peel:

> 6 medium potatoes

Steam for about 15 minutes or until soft. Place the potatoes in a bowl, and mash with a little water or soymilk.

Preheat the oven to 350°F.

Line the bottom of a lightly oiled pie pan with the mashed potatoes. Put the following mixture on top of the potatoes:

> 1 pound tofu, mashed
> 2 teaspoons Herb Mix (page 98)
> 1 cup chopped onions
> 1 cup chopped celery
> 1 cup chopped carrots

Sprinkle on top:

> 1 slice whole wheat bread, crumbled
> Fresh chopped parsley

Bake for 15 minutes.

| Per Serving: | |
|---|---|
| **Exchanges** | |
| 3 starch, 1 vegetable, 1 meat | |
| Calories | 314 |
| Total Fat | 6 g |
| % of calories from fat | 17% |
| Saturated Fat | 1 g |
| Protein | 15 g |
| Carbohydrate | 54 g |
| Fiber | 28 g |
| Sodium | 82 mg |
| Calcium | 164 mg |

# Tofu-Mushroom Pot Pies

Yield: 4 servings

*You can make these up on the weekend and refrigerate them, and warm them up one at a time throughout the week for a quick-fix lunch or dinner.*

To make the crust, mix together with a fork:

> 1¼ cups whole wheat pastry flour
> ¼ cup wheat germ
> 3 tablespoons oil
> 2 to 3 tablespoons water

Divide into 4 pieces, roll out individually, and place each piece in an ovenproof dish.

To make the filling, simmer for 10 minutes:

> 2 cups chopped mushrooms
> 1 cup chopped celery with leaves
> ½ cup chopped onion
> 1 tablespoon salt-free vegetable
>     bouillon powder
> ½ cup water

Preheat the oven to 350°F.

Stir into the mixture:

> ½ cups diced tofu

Divide the filling among the 4 dishes, and bake for 30 minutes.

| Per Serving: | |
|---|---|
| **Exchanges** | |
| 2 starch, 1 vegetable, 2 fat, 1 meat | |
| Calories | 355 |
| Total Fat | 17 g |
| % of calories from fat | 43% |
| Saturated Fat | 2 g |
| Protein | 16 g |
| Carbohydrate | 37 g |
| Fiber | 8 g |
| Sodium | 35 mg |
| Calcium | 110 mg |

# Meatless Loaf

Yield: 4 servings

*Textured soy protein granules provide the perfect texture for this traditional favorite.*

Mix and set aside for 15 minutes:

>   1½ cups textured soy protein granules (See.page 50.)
>   1 teaspoon basil
>   ½ teaspoon garlic powder
>   ½ teaspoon oregano
>   ¼ cup fresh chopped parsley
>   ¼ teaspoon salt
>   1 cup whole wheat bread crumbs
>   1½ cups boiling water
>   ¼ cup tomato sauce

Preheat the oven to 350°F.

Sauté:

>   ½ cup chopped onion
>   1 tablespoon olive oil

Add the sautéed onion to the mixture, and bake in a nonstick pan for 20 minutes.

| Per Serving: | |
|---|---|
| **Exchanges** | |
| 2 meat, 1 starch, 1 fat | |
| Calories | 170 |
| Total Fat | 4 g |
| % of calories from fat | 21% |
| Saturated Fat | 1 g |
| Protein | 16 g |
| Carbohydrate | 17 g |
| Fiber | 4 g |
| Sodium | 294 mg |
| Calcium | 93 mg |

# Vegetable Medley with Pasta

Yield: 3 servings

*The emphasis here is on the vegetables. A light sauce and colorful pasta make this quick meal seem like a real feast. You can substitute tofu for the textured soy. (This dish is pictured on the cover.)*

Cook until al dente:

>    10 ounces tri-colored bowtie pasta

Steam in a saucepan just until crisp tender:

>    ½ cup chopped broccoli
>    ½ cup chopped red bell pepper
>    ½ cup diagonally sliced carrots
>    ½ cup diagonally sliced green beans
>    ¼ cup sliced water chestnuts
>    ¼ cup snow peas

Boil for 10 minutes or until tender:

>    ½ cup water
>    ¼ cup chicken-style textured soy
>       protein chunks (See page 50.)

Lightly coat a nonstick pan with oil spray, and sauté the textured soy concentrate chunks for 3 minutes over low heat. Add:

>    ½ teaspoon tamari

| Per Serving: | |
|---|---|
| **Exchanges** | |
| 2 starches, 1 meat, 1 vegetable | |
| Calories | 218 |
| Total Fat | 1 g |
| % of calories from fat | 4% |
| Saturated Fat | 0 g |
| Protein | 16 g |
| Carbohydrate | 38 g |
| Fiber | 9 g |
| Sodium | 90 mg |
| Calcium | 92 mg |

Stir and cook for 1 more minute, and remove from the heat.

Toss the pasta, vegetables, and soy chunks together, and serve with your favorite vegetable sauce.

# Falafel

Yield: 4 servings

*These little grain balls are usually served in pita pockets. They are fabulous with a little tahini or miso sauce, sprouts and tomatoes.*

Grind in a food processor or blender:

> 3 cups cooked garbanzo beans
> 1 tablespoon lemon juice
> ½ cup chopped onion

Remove and mix with:

> 2 tablespoons whole wheat pastry flour
> ¼ cup wheat germ
> ¼ cup parsley
> 2 tablespoons sesame seed
> ¼ teaspoon pepper
> ¼ teaspoon garlic powder

Form the mixture into 20 balls.

Preheat the oven to 350°F. Heat in a large baking dish while the oven is preheating:

> 2 teaspoons oil

Place the falafel balls in the dish, and bake for 15 minutes, stirring occasionally.

| Per Serving: | |
|---|---|
| **Exchanges** | |
| 2 starch, 1 meat, 1 fat | |
| Calories | 275 |
| Total Fat | 8 g |
| % of calories from fat | 25% |
| Saturated Fat | 1 g |
| Protein | 14 g |
| Carbohydrate | 38 g |
| Fiber | 10 g |
| Sodium | 20 mg |
| Calcium | 107 mg |

# Hearty Beans & Rice

Yield: 4 servings

*Although it's not necessary to eat beans and rice at the same meal, it's still a complete protein combination that tastes great, especially in cold weather.*

Simmer over low heat for 35 minutes:

⅔ cup brown rice
1½ cups water
1 cup chopped celery
½ cup chopped onion
½ cup chopped green bell pepper
½ teaspoon ground bay leaves
½ teaspoon basil
½ teaspoon oregano

Mix in:

2 cups cooked pinto beans
1 cup fresh or frozen corn
2 fresh tomatoes, chopped
1 teaspoon olive oil

Cook for another 10 minutes.

| Per Serving: | |
|---|---|
| **Exchanges** | |
| 1 meat, 1 vegetable, 2 starch | |
| Calories | 269 |
| Total Fat | 3 g |
| % of calories from fat | 10% |
| Saturated Fat | 0 g |
| Protein | 11 g |
| Carbohydrate | 53 g |
| Fiber | 11 g |
| Sodium | 40 mg |
| Calcium | 69 mg |

# Pintos with Cornbread Topping

Yield: 4 servings

*You can try reversing this and using the topping on the bottom and the beans on top. Either way it's great!*

Simmer over medium heat for 10 minutes:

> 3 cups cooked pinto beans
> ⅓ cup tomato sauce
> ⅓ cup chopped onion
> ⅓ cup chopped green bell pepper

Preheat the oven to 400°F.

For the topping, mix in a small bowl:

> 4 teaspoons canola oil
> 1 cup cornmeal
> 1 cup low-fat soymilk
> 1 teaspoon chili powder (optional)

Put the beans in an 8 x 8-inch dish, then pour the cornmeal mixture on top. Bake for 15 to 20 minutes, uncovered.

| Per Serving: | |
|---|---|
| **Exchanges** | |
| 2½ meat, 2 bread, 1 fat | |
| Calories | 367 |
| Total Fat | 7 g |
| % of calories from fat | 17% |
| Saturated Fat | 1 g |
| Protein | 14 g |
| Carbohydrate | 64 g |
| Fiber | 14 g |
| Sodium | 153 mg |
| Calcium | 75 mg |

# Walnut-Lentil Loaf

Yield: 4 servings

*Curry powder to taste can be used in place of thyme, basil, and oregano.*

Have ready:

> 1 slice whole wheat bread, crumbled
> 2 cups cooked lentils

Process in a blender:

> ⅓ cup walnuts
> ½ cup onions
> ½ cup water

Preheat the oven to 350°F.

Mix together the above ingredients in the order given with:

> ½ cup wheat germ
> ½ teaspoon thyme
> ¼ teaspoon basil
> ¼ teaspoon oregano
> 2 tablespoons nutritional yeast flakes
> ½ cup water
> 1 tablespoon tomato sauce

Place the mixture in a small loaf pan or in an 8 x 8-inch dish coated with:

> ½ teaspoon oil

Bake for 35 to 40 minutes.

| Per Serving: | |
|---|---|
| **Exchanges** | |
| 1 fat, 2 starch, 1 meat | |
| Calories | 263 |
| Total Fat | 8 g |
| % of calories from fat | 28% |
| Saturated Fat | 1 g |
| Protein | 18 g |
| Carbohydrate | 34 g |
| Fiber | 11 g |
| Sodium | 54 mg |
| Calcium | 37 mg |

# Vegetables

# Lemon-Garlic Asparagus

Yield: 3 servings

*Fresh asparagus is always a delight. Lightly steaming until just crisp-tender brings out its rich green color without destroying the vitamins.*

In a nonstick frying pan, place:

> 3 tablespoons water
> 1 pound fresh asparagus stalks with the tough ends removed

Cover and steam until crisp-tender, about 4 minutes.
Remove the lid and sprinkle over:

> ¼ teaspoon fresh lemon juice
> 2 tablespoons minced garlic
> Pinch of salt

Lightly spritz with:

> Olive oil cooking spray (optional)

Simmer for 2 minutes. Remove from the pan and serve hot.

| Per Serving: | |
|---|---|
| **Exchanges** | |
| 2 vegetable | |
| Calories | 54 |
| Total Fat | 1 g |
| % of calories from fat | 16% |
| Saturated Fat | 0 g |
| Protein | 5 g |
| Carbohydrate | 10 g |
| Fiber | 34 g |
| Sodium | 19 mg |
| Calcium | 52 mg |

# Broccoli-Mushroom Casserole

Yield: 4 servings

*With dishes as filling as this one, you can see how a person could live on vegetables and plant foods—and love it! Try this recipe with different kinds of mushrooms to get the flavor and texture you want.*

Preheat the oven to 350°F.

Bring to a boil:

> 1 cup water

Add:

> 2 cups chopped broccoli
> 2 cups chopped mushrooms
> ½ cup chopped onion
> 2 cloves garlic, minced

Simmer for 3 minutes. Add:

> 2 cups brown rice or quinoa
> ¼ cup sesame seeds
> ½ pound tofu, mashed

Mix together well. Put into an oiled baking dish, and bake for 15 minutes. Top with:

> ½ cup tomato sauce

Bake for 5 minutes more and serve.

| Per Serving: | |
|---|---|
| **Exchanges** | |
| 2 meat, 1 bread, 2 vegetable | |
| Calories | 288 |
| Total Fat | 10 g |
| % of calories from fat | 31% |
| Saturated Fat | 2 g |
| Protein | 15 g |
| Carbohydrate | 38 g |
| Fiber | 9 g |
| Sodium | 205 mg |
| Calcium | 199 mg |

# Dairy-Free Scalloped Potatoes

Yield: 6 servings

*If you like potatoes, you'll enjoy this full-bodied casserole.*

Sauté together:

> 1 teaspoon olive oil
> 1 large onion, sliced
> 4 cloves garlic, minced

Add:

> 1½ cups water
> ¼ cup tahini
> 2 tablespoons whole wheat flour
> 1 teaspoon salt (optional)

Stir until thick.

Steam for 15 minutes or until soft:

> 6 to 7 medium potatoes, sliced

Preheat the oven to 350°F.

Layer the potatoes in a casserole dish, and pour the onion/tahini mixture over the top. Sprinkle with:

> 2 tablespoons chopped parsley

Cook uncovered for 10 to 15 minutes.

| Per Serving: | |
|---|---|
| **Exchanges** | |
| 2 starch, 1 fat | |
| Calories | 215 |
| Total Fat | 6 g |
| % of calories from fat | 25% |
| Saturated Fat | 1 g |
| Protein | 5 g |
| Carbohydrate | 37 g |
| Fiber | 5 g |
| Sodium | 15 mg |
| Calcium | 60 mg |

# Sesame Potatoes

Yield: 4 servings

*This dish is easy to prepare and makes a good companion for the Meatless Loaf on page 129. Use a nonstick pan for the first part of this recipe.*

Steam until almost done:

    2 cups diced potatoes (with skins)
    1 cup fresh peas (If 1 cup frozen peas are substituted, they do not need to be cooked.)

Preheat the oven to 350°F.

Mix in:

    2 tablespoons chopped onion
    1 tablespoon chopped parsley
    1 cup crumbled tofu
    2 tablespoons sesame seeds

Place in a lightly oiled 8 x 8-inch casserole, and top with:

    3 tablespoons soy Parmesan
    1 tablespoon sesame seeds

Bake uncovered for 30 minutes.

| Per Serving: | |
|---|---|
| **Exchanges** | |
| 2 starch, 1 meat, 1 fat | |
| Calories | 252 |
| Total Fat | 7 g |
|   % of calories from fat | 25% |
|   Saturated Fat | 1 g |
| Protein | 13 g |
| Carbohydrate | 37 g |
| Fiber | 6 g |
| Sodium | 109 mg |
| Calcium | 189 mg |

# Sweet Potato Rice

Yield: 2 servings

*Sweet potatoes are highly nutritious, and their bright color
and distinctive flavor make this an appealing dish.*

Cover and cook over low heat for 40 minutes:

⅔ cup brown rice
2 cups water

Stir in and heat thoroughly:

2 tablespoons chopped fresh parsley
¼ teaspoon sage
½ cup cooked, mashed sweet potatoes
¼ teaspoon pepper
¼ teaspoon wheat germ
1 tablespoon nutritional yeast flakes

Serve warm or cold topped with:

½ cup soy yogurt

| Per Serving: | |
|---|---|
| **Exchanges** | |
| 3 starch | |
| Calories | 256 |
| Total Fat | 3 g |
| % of calories from fat | 10% |
| Saturated Fat | 0 g |
| Protein | 9 g |
| Carbohydrate | 50 g |
| Fiber | 5 g |
| Sodium | 24 mg |
| Calcium | 47 mg |

# Sweet Potatoes & Broccoli

Yield: 1 serving

*Here's a really quick way to combine these two vegetables in a single dish.*

Cook in a covered saucepan until almost done:

> 1 medium sweet potato or yam, diced
> ½ cup water

Add and cook until tender:

> 1 cup chopped fresh broccoli
> Additional water to cook, if necessary

Toss in with the vegetables:

> ¼ cup crumbled tofu
> 1 teaspoon sesame seeds

Cook until heated through.

| Per Serving: | |
|---|---|
| **Exchanges** | |
| 2 starch, 1 vegetable, 1 fat, 1 meat | |
| Calories | 268 |
| Total Fat | 8 g |
| % of calories from fat | 26% |
| Saturated Fat | 1 g |
| Protein | 17 g |
| Carbohydrate | 39 g |
| Fiber | 10 g |
| Sodium | 62 mg |
| Calcium | 236 mg |

# Baked Diced Potatoes

Yield: 1 serving

*Add a little interest to your baked potatoes with this preparation method.*

Preheat the oven to 375°F.

Place in a small casserole dish:

> 1 cup diced potatoes

Add:

> 1 tablespoon water
> 1 tablespoon apple cider vinegar
> ¼ teaspoon dill
> ¼ teaspoon oregano
> ⅛ teaspoon pepper

Stir to coat the potatoes. Cover the dish and bake for 20 minutes.

| Per Serving: | |
|---|---|
| **Exchanges** | |
| 2 starch | |
| Calories | 120 |
| Total Fat | 0 g |
| % of calories from fat | 0% |
| Saturated Fat | 0 g |
| Protein | 3 g |
| Carbohydrate | 28 g |
| Fiber | 3 g |
| Sodium | 6 mg |
| Calcium | 8 mg |

# Golden Yeast Sauce

Yield: 2½ cups (10 servings)

*Nutritional yeast flakes add a golden color, great flavor, and nutrition to this gravy. Try it with toast points or biscuits, or pour it on your favorite pasta and vegetables.*

Combine in a saucepan:

 ⅓ cup nutritional yeast flakes
 ⅓ cup whole wheat pastry flour
 2 cups water

Cook over low heat until bubbling. Remove from the heat.

Add:

 1 tablespoon olive oil
 1 teaspoon prepared mustard

For a darker sauce, mix the flour and yeast in a saucepan, and brown first.

| Per Serving: | |
|---|---|
| **Exchanges** | |
| ½ starch | |
| Calories | 34 |
| Total Fat | 1 g |
| % of calories from fat | 26% |
| Saturated Fat | 0 g |
| Protein | 2 g |
| Carbohydrate | 4 g |
| Fiber | 0 g |
| Sodium | 19 mg |
| Calcium | 3 mg |

# Cheezy Bechamel Sauce

Yield: 2 cups (8 servings)

*This all-purpose white sauce can be used over potatoes, pasta, or any grain.*

Melt in a heavy-bottomed saucepan over medium heat:

> 2 teaspoons oil

Mix in:

> ⅓ cup whole wheat pastry flour
> ⅓ cup soy Parmesan
> 2 tablespoons Herb Mix (page 98)

Slowly add:

> 2 cups low-fat soymilk

Stir until thick and creamy.

| Per Serving: | |
|---|---|
| **Exchanges** | |
| ¼ fat, ¼ starch, ¼ meat, ¼ milk | |
| Calories | 72 |
| Total Fat | 2 g |
| % of calories from fat | 25% |
| Saturated Fat | 0 g |
| Protein | 4 g |
| Carbohydrate | 10 g |
| Fiber | 1 g |
| Sodium | 108 mg |
| Calcium | 40 mg |

Desserts
and Snacks

# Chocolate Cake

Yield: one (10-inch) cake
(16 servings)

*This is the delicious cake pictured on the cover.*

Preheat the oven to 350°F. In a bowl, combine:

> 2 cups whole wheat pastry flour
> 1½ teaspoons baking soda
> ¼ teaspoon salt
> ⅓ cup cocoa
> 1¼ cups sugar

Mix well. In another bowl, combine:

> 6 tablespoons canola oil
> 1⅓ cups low-fat soymilk
> 2 teaspoons vanilla

Blend together:

> 2 tablespoons ground flaxseeds
> 3 tablespoons water

Add to the liquid mixture, and stir.
Combine the wet and dry ingredients, and
mix well. Stir in:

> 1 tablespoon white vinegar

| Per Serving: | |
|---|---|
| **Exchanges** | |
| 2 starch, 1 fat | |
| Calories | 200 |
| Total Fat | 6 g |
| % of calories from fat | 31% |
| Saturated Fat | 1 g |
| Protein | 3 g |
| Carbohydrate | 29 g |
| Fiber | 3 g |
| Sodium | 40 mg |
| Calcium | 8 mg |

Pour the mixture into an oiled, 10-inch, springform cake pan, and bake for 35 minutes. Cool for 15 minutes and remove from the pan. Be sure to cool the cake completely before icing.

# Creamy Chocolate Icing

Yield: 16 servings

*This lite, firm icing will give any cake an elegant look. Just make sure the cake is completely cooled and ready for the icing before you make it.*

Microwave in a glass measuring cup until softened, about 1 minute:

> 10 ounces semisweet chocolate chips, melted

Combine the melted chocolate chips in a food processor with:

> 10 ounces lite, firm silken tofu
> ½ teaspoon vanilla

To make the icing with a blender, mash the tofu in a bowl with the vanilla. Stir the melted chips and mix into the tofu. Immediately blend in two batches. Turn off the blender and scrape down the sides several times until both batches are smooth and creamy. Mix them in a bowl

Spread on the cooled cake immediately.

| Per Serving: | |
|---|---|
| **Exchanges** | |
| 1 starch | |
| Calories | 99 |
| Total Fat | 5 g |
| % of calories from fat | 45% |
| Saturated Fat | 0 g |
| Protein | 3 g |
| Carbohydrate | 11 g |
| Fiber | 0 g |
| Sodium | 17 mg |
| Calcium | 10 mg |

# Five-Fruit Salad

Yield: 4 servings

*A little fruit salad makes a light, tasty, energizing breakfast.*
*This one is especially good as a source of vitamin C.*

Toss together:

    4 fresh apricots or plums, pitted and cut up,
        or 1 cup seedless grapes
    ½ cup fresh raspberries
    1 orange, peeled and cut into wedges
    1 cup fresh diced pineapple
    1 banana, sliced
    2 teaspoons lemon juice

| **Per Serving:** | |
|---|---:|
| **Exchanges** | |
| 1 fruit | |
| Calories | 86 |
| Total Fat | 1 g |
| % of calories from fat | 10% |
| Saturated Fat | 0 g |
| Protein | 1 g |
| Carbohydrate | 21 g |
| Fiber | 4 g |
| Sodium | 1 mg |
| Calcium | 26 mg |

# Northern Fruit Salad

Yield: 4 servings

*Here is a combination of fruits that are relatively easy to find in whatever part of the country you may be living.*

Toss together:

    2 medium apples, diced
    2 medium pears, diced
    10 cherries, pitted
    10 seedless  grapes
    2 teaspoons lemon juice

| Per Serving: | |
|---|---|
| **Exchanges** | |
| 2 fruit | |
| Calories | 107 |
| Total Fat | 1 g |
| % of calories from fat | 8% |
| Saturated Fat | 0 g |
| Protein | 1 g |
| Carbohydrate | 27 g |
| Fiber | 5 g |
| Sodium | 0 mg |
| Calcium | 18 mg |

# Apple-Oat Drop Cookies

Yield: 20 cookies

*This variation of the traditional oatmeal cookie gets natural sweetness from the apples and raisins in the recipe.*

Mash together with a fork:

> 1½ cups rolled oats
> 1 tablespoon whole wheat flour
> 2 medium apples, grated
> 1 tablespoon oil
> ½ teaspoon vanilla
> ¼ cup water

Mix in:

> ½ cup raisins
> ¼ cup finely chopped walnuts

Preheat the oven to 350°F.

Let the mixture soak together in the bowl for 15 minutes. Drop by tablespoons onto an ungreased baking sheet. Bake for 10 to 12 minutes.

| Per Cookie: | |
|---|---|
| **Exchanges** | |
| ½ bread, 1 fat | |
| Calories | 60 |
| Total Fat | 2 g |
| % of calories from fat | 30% |
| Saturated Fat | 1 g |
| Protein | 1 g |
| Carbohydrate | 10 g |
| Fiber | 2 g |
| Sodium | 1 mg |
| Calcium | 7 mg |

# Quick Rice Pudding

Yield: 2 servings

*Although brown rice is mostly used in savory dishes,
it's also delicious as a sweet dessert treat.*

Preheat the oven to 350°F.

Mix together in the order given:

> 1 cup cooked brown rice
> ¾ cup low-fat soymilk
> 1½ tablespoons raisins
> 2 teaspoons maple syrup

Divide into 2 small serving dishes, and sprinkle with:

> ¼ teaspoon cinnamon
> ½ teaspoon vanilla

Bake for 15 minutes, and refrigerate before serving.

| Per Serving: | |
|---|---|
| **Exchanges** | |
| 2 starch | |
| Calories | 177 |
| Total Fat | 2 g |
| % of calories from fat | 9% |
| Saturated Fat | 0 g |
| Protein | 4 g |
| Carbohydrate | 37 g |
| Fiber | 3 g |
| Sodium | 33 mg |
| Calcium | 91 mg |

# *Popcorn*

Yield: 1 serving

*This is a good snack for a person with diabetes because of the large, satisfying quantity that is allowed for 1 bread exchange. (One-third cup unpopped popcorn will equal 3 cups popped for 90 calories and 1 bread exchange.) Without butter or salt, it is low in calories and provides good roughage and some trace minerals. Here are some other ingredients which can be added to popcorn to create new snack ideas.*

Have ready:

>   3 cups popped popcorn

Mix in:

>   2 tablespoons soy Parmesan
>   1 tablespoon peanuts

*Variation: For a really unique and tasty combination, sprinkle on:*

>   1 tablespoon nutritional yeast

| Per Serving: | |
|---|---|
| **Exchanges** | |
| 1 meat, 1 fat, 1 starch | |
| Calories | 214 |
| Total Fat | 6 g |
| % of calories from fat | 27% |
| Saturated Fat | 1 g |
| Protein | 15 g |
| Carbohydrate | 26 g |
| Fiber | 5 g |
| Sodium | 258 mg |
| Calcium | 115 mg |

# BOOK PUBLISHING COMPANY

*since 1974—books that educate, inspire, and empower*

Book Publishing Co.
P.O. Box 99
Summertown, TN 38483
800-695-2241

*Look for these other books at your local bookstore
or you can order directly from the publisher.*
*(Please add $3.95 per book for shipping and handling.)*
*Call for a free catalog.*

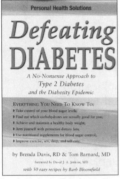

Defeating Diabetes
Brenda Davis, RD &
Tom Barnard, MD
$14.95

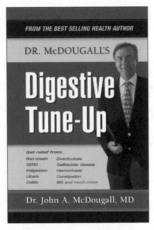

Dr. McDougall's
Digestive Tune-Up
John McDougall, MD
$19.95

Stevia
Naturally Sweet Recipes for
Desserts, Drinks & More!
Rita DePuydt
$14.95

The Pleasure Trap
Doug Lisle, PhD & Alan Goldhamer, DC
$12.95

The Health-Promoting Cookbook
Alan Goldhamer, DC
$12.95

Find your favorite vegetarian food products and books online at www.healthy-eating.com